John Warburton, Andrew Coltee Ducarel

Some Account of the Alien Priories

and of such lands as they are known to have possessed in England and Wales - Vol.

2

John Warburton, Andrew Coltee Ducarel

Some Account of the Alien Priories
and of such lands as they are known to have possessed in England and Wales - Vol. 2

ISBN/EAN: 9783337220754

Printed in Europe, USA, Canada, Australia, Japan

Cover: Foto ©Andreas Hilbeck / pixelio.de

More available books at **www.hansebooks.com**

SOME ACCOUNT

OF THE

ALIEN PRIORIES,

AND

OF SUCH LANDS

AS THEY ARE KNOWN TO HAVE POSSESSED

IN

ENGLAND AND WALES,

Collected from the MSS. of JOHN WAR-
BURTON, Esq. and Dr. DUCAREL.

A NEW EDITION,

IN TWO VOLUMES.

VOLUME THE SECOND.

LONDON,

PRINTED BY AND FOR J. NICHOLS:
AND SOLD BY C. DILLY, IN THE POULTRY.
MDCCLXXXVI.

LIST OF ALIEN PRIORIES IN THE SECOND VOLUME.

Angers, 64.
Beauport, 52.
Begard, 129.
Bellencombre, 36.
St. Benoit fur Loire, 112.
St. Bertin, 111.
Blanche Lande, 11.
St. Carilef, vulgò St. Calais, 100.
La Charité, 108.
Charleval, 41.
Chaſtillon, 120.
Cheſay, 13.
Cherbourg, 14. 53.
Ciſteaux, 87.
Clairvaux, 94.
Clugny, 104.
Corneville, 22.
St. Denys, 117.
Les Emmurées, 42 *.
Fleury, 21. 112.
St. Florant de Saumur, 78.
Fontevrault, 69. 75 *.
Fontenelle, or St. Vandrille, 18.

Fougeres, 122.
St. Fremont, 7.
Gaille Fontaine, 29.
St. George at Bocherville, 33.
Grandmont, Evreux, 43.
——— Limoiſin, 96.
——— Rouen, 30.
Hambie, 3.
St. Jacut, or Jagu, 92.
Leſſay, 5.
Liſieux, 48.
Livray, 51.
St. Lo, Coutance, 40.
——— Rouen, 12.
St. Lucien, 83.
Marmoutier, 131.
St. Martin aux Jumeaux, 61.
——— d'Acy, 37.
——— des Champs, 114.
St. Maurice d'Angers, 82.
St. Melaine, 123.

Vol. II.   b   Mont

Mont aux Malades, 29.
Montier Neuf, 121.
Montebourg, 8.
Nanteuil, 13.
Neumarche, 42.
St. Nicaife de Meulant, 89.
Notre Dame de bonnes Nouvelles, Rouen, 23.
La Perrine, 12.
Perſeigne, 99.
St. Peter at Ghent, 127.
—— at Rome, 139.
St. Remy, 125.
Raviers, 49.
La Foie de Notre Dame, 39.

S. Sauveur Evreux, 46.
—— le Vicomte, 4.
Seauve Majeur, 85.
S. Sever, 1.
S. Sierge, 75.
Tiron, 90.
La Sainte Trinité du Mont, 25.
S. Valery, 62.
Vernon, 47.
Vienne, 135.
Villers, 49.
—— St. Maria, 50.
St. Victor, 113.
St. Vincent, 102.

CONTENTS OF APPENDIX.

I. Account of Priories Alien belonging to King's College, Cambridge, referring to the first edition of Tanner's Notitia Monastica, from the Harleian MSS. 7048, p. 141.

II. Lands and possessions of Alien Priories given by Henry VI. to the colleges of Eton and Cambridge, 150. 157.

III. Forms of Indenization of Alien Priories, 161. Petition of Thetford Abbey to be made Denizon, 161. Indenization of the Benedictine Priory of St. Trinity, York, 167.

IV. Form of restoring lands of Alien Priories, 172.

V. Form of seizing lands of Alien Priories, 182.

VI. Another Form of restoring lands of Alien Priories, 192.

VII. Licence to an Alien Priory made to alienate lands, 196.

VIII. A third form of restoring Alien Priory lands to Henry IV. 201.

IX. Act for suppressing the Alien Priories, 211.

X. Alien Priories granted in fee, 217.

XI. Pro Decano & Capitulo Ecclesiæ Rothomagensis, super dono & concessione Edwardi Confessoris, 224.

Add to p. 59.

Osbert Fitz Hugh, elder brother of Hugh de Say of Richard's Castle, and grandson of Osbern Fitz Richards, gave to the monks of *Font Evraud*, in Normandy, Westwood, together with the church of Coderugge and other possessions. Dr. Nash, Worcestershire, vol. I. p. 258, from Mon. Ang. vol. I. p. 574. b. 868. a. 975. b.

SOME ACCOUNT

OF THE

ALIEN PRIORIES.

DIOCESE OF COUTANCE.

S. SEVERUS.

S. SEVER.

A Benedictine abbey in a town of that name; founded (as supposed) by Severus bishop of Avranches, about A. D. 558.

This monastery was refounded about 1085, by Hugo de Abrincis, viscount d'Avranches, afterwards earl of Chester.

Annual income between 8 and 9000 livres.

See Monaſt. Angl. tom. II. p. 950. 25. 1002. b.

Neuſtria Pia, p. 74.

At Hagham in Lincolnſhire was an eſtate and priory belonging to this abbey. Tanner's Notitia, p. 281.

At Endeſton in Somerſetſhire was an alien priory of Benedictine Monks, cell to this abbey. Ib. p. 475.

Rot. Vaſconiæ anno 13 E. I. m. 13. De compoſitione inter regem ſeu gentes ſuas et abbatem et conventum Sancti Severi ſuper juſtitia ejuſdem loci obſervanda. Teſte Rege apud Weſtminſter 13 Junii.

Rot. Patent. Normann. de anno 6 H. V. pars 1. m. 11. De cuſtodia
tem-

temporalium abbatiæ de Saint Sever, commissa religiosis viris ibidem.

HAMBEYA.

HAMBIE.

A Benedictine abbey in a town of that name; founded A. D. 1145, by William Paisnel lord of this manor.

Annual income 9000 livres.

See Neustria Pia, p. 821.

Rot. Normann. de anno 7 H. V. p. 1. m. . De temporalibus restitutis monasterio B. M. de Hambye.

S. SALVATOR.

S. SAUVEUR LE VICOMTE.

An abbey of Benedictine monks, in a town of that name; founded A. D. 1048, by Nigellus lord of this town, and viscount of Cotentin.

See Monast. Angl. tom. II. p. 950. 59. 1001. b.

Neustria Pia, p. 540.

The tithes of the parish church of All Saints, with the chapel of St. Mary at Elingham, in Hampshire, were the first and chief endowment of an alien priory belonging to this abbey. Tanner's Notitia, p. 163.

EXAQUIUM.

MONASTERIUM S. TRINITATIS EXAQUII.

LESSAY.

A Benedictine abbey founded by Turstin Halduc and Emma his wife, A. D. 1064.

Annual income 26000 livres.

See Monast. Angl. tom. II. p. 950. 968. a.

Neustria Pia, p. 617.

Rot. Normann. de anno 8 Hen. V. pars II. m. 21. De confirmatione cartarum pro monachis de Exaquio.

At Boxgrove in Sussex was an alien priory subordinate to this abbey, val. £.145. 10s. 2d. per ann. See Tanner's Notitia, p. 555.

Buck

Buck engraved a N. W. view of its ruins, 1737, and Grose another, 1761.

Rot. Lit. Patent. Normann. de anno 6 H. V. pars 1. m. 35. De custodia temporalium abbatiæ Sanctæ Trinitatis de Lessay in diocesi de Coutances, commissa religiosis viris ibidem.

Patent. Normann. de anno 6 Hen. V. pars 2. m. 35. Rex concessit abbati et conventui abbatiæ Sti. Trinitatis de l'Essay omnia temporalia sua.

Rot. Normann. de anno 6 H. V. pars II. m. 30. dorso. De potestate commissa Johanni de Aston, ad exigendum sacramentum fidelitatis nomine regis de abbate Sti. Trinitatis de Lessay.

S. FREMONDUS.
S. FREMONT.

St. Fremont is a town situate upon the river Vire; wherein is a priory, whose prior had formerly a seat in the exchequer of Normandy.

See Etat Geographique de Normandie, par Masseville, vol. I. p. 286.

Pat. 3 H. IV. part I. m. 30.

Rot. Normann. de anno 7 H. V. pars I. m. 78. De temporalibus restitutis prioratui beatæ Mariæ de Sancto Fremondo.

See a composition between the monks of St. Fremond and the nuns of Stamford, touching the church of All Saints in the town of Stamford, (sans date) printed in Madox's Formulare, N° XLIII.

MONS BURGUS.

MONTISBURGENSE COENOBIUM.

MONTEBOURG.

A Benedictine abbey in a town of that name; founded A. D. 1090, and mproved by the lords de Redvers.

Annual income 20000 livres.

See Monaftic. Angl. tom. II. p.951. 4. 992. a.

Neuftria Pia, p. 672.

Rot. Lit. Pat. Normann. de anno 6 Hen. V. pars 1. m. 35. De temporalibus reftitutis abbatiæ de Mountebourg in patria Coftentin.

Rot. Normann. de anno 10 H. V. m. 13. De confirmatione cartarum pro abbate Montifburgi.

The

MONTEBOURG.   DIOCESE OF COUTANCE

The manor of Apeldercomb, or Apple Durwell, in the Isle of Wight, belonged to this abbey. Tanner's Notitia, p. 168.

At Lodres in Dorsetshire was an alien priory, subordinate to this abbey, to which the manor of Lodres was given by Benedict, or Richard de Redvers, temp. Hen. I. on which account the abbat of that foreign monastery was prebendary in the cathedral church of Salisbury, and had a house in the close there. This priory was valued at £.80 per ann. and was given by Henry V, 1414, to the nunnery of Sion, Middlesex. Tanner's Notitia, p. 106. Hutchins's Dorset, I. 356.

The manor of Axmouth, in the deanry of Honiton in Devonshire, being given to this abbey by Richard de Redvers or Rivers, earl of Devonshire, temp. Hen. II. it was reckoned sometimes as a distinct alien priory; at other times, as parcel of Lodres. Tanner's Notitia, p. 94. Hutchins ubi sup.

BLANCA

BLANCHE LANDE. DIOCESE OF COUTANCE.

BLANCA LANDA.

ABBATIA DE BLANCA LANDA.

BLANCHE LANDE.

An abbey of Premonstratensians; founded A. D. 1155, by Richard baron de la Haye, constable of Normandy. Its annual income 6000 livres.

See Mon. Angl. tom. II. p. 1015. a. Neustria Pia, p. 842.

At Cameringham in Lincolnshire was an alien priory belonging to this abbey. Tanner's Notitia, p. 272.

PERRINA.
LA PERRINE.

A priory of the order of the Mathurins; founded A. D. 1250, by Euſtatia wife of William du Hommet conſtable of Normandy. Annual income 4000 livres.

See Neuſtria Pia, p. 913.

S. LAUDUS.
ST. LO.

An abbey of Regular Canons of St. Auſtin, in a town of the ſame name, ſituate on the river Vire, founded A. D. 1150.

See Neuſtria Pia, p. 836.

Rot. Normann. de anno 5 H. V. m. 37. Pro abbatia de St. Lo, de reſtitutione temporalium.

NANTUS.

NANTEUIL.

An abbey of Benedictines, said to have been founded A. D. 558, by St. Marculphus, who was buried there; but on the destruction of this house by the Normans, removed to Mantes.

See Neustria Pia, p. 69. 72.

SISCIACUM.

CHESAY.

A Benedictine abbey, said to have been founded A. D. 550, by St. Paternus.

See Neustria Pia, p. 66.

CÆSARIS-BURGUS, seu DE VOTO.
CHERBOURG, N. DAME DU VOEU.

An abbey of Regular Canons of St. Auftin, founded A. D. 1145, by the emprefs Matilda, in confequence of a vow to the Bleffed Virgin, if fhe got fafe to England on the death of her father Henry I.

Her fon, Henry II. was acknowledged a co-founder.

See Monafticon, tom. II. p. 1008.

Neuftria Pia, p. 813.

About A. D. 1164, king Henry II. gave to this abbey the manor of Hagh, Halgh, or Howghe, on the Mount, in Lincolnfhire, fo that there was an alien priory of fome Auftin Canons fubordinate to that foreign monaftery. Tanner's Notitia, p. 272.

The

The priory of St. Helier in Jersey, was appropriated to the abbey de Voto at Cherbourg, and fell to the crown with the rest of the incomes of the Alien Priories. Hist. of Jersey, by P. Falle, ed. 1734, 8vo.

Rot. Patent. Normann. de anno 6 H. V. pars 1. m. 6. De temporalibus restitutis religiosis viris abbatiæ Beatæ Mariæ de Vœu prope Cherbourg.

Rot. Normann. de anno 6 H. V. pars 1. m. 6. De temporalibus restitutis religiosis viris abbatiæ Beatæ Mariæ de Vœu prope Cherbourg.

Rot. Normann. de anno 6 H. V. pars 2. m. 29. Rex adhibuit assensum electioni factæ in ecclesia conventuali beatæ Mariæ de Voto juxta Cæsaris-Burgum.

Rot.

Rot. Franciæ de anno 10 Ricardi II. m. 1. De cuſtodia Prioratus de Hagh in comitatu de Lincoln, ac Prioratus de Sancto Helier in inſula de Jerſey, conceſſa abbati et conventui de Voto juxta Cherbourg in Normannia fundato per Regem Henricum II. Teſte Rege apud caſtrum de Notingham, 21 Februarii.

Rot. Franciæ de anno 3 Ric. II. m. 27. De concedendo abbati et conventui de Voto juxta Chierbourg in Normannia (fundato per Henricum II.) cuſtodiam Prioratus de Hagh in comitatu de Lincoln, ac Prioratus de Saint Helyer in Inſula Jerſey. Teſte R. apud Weſtminſter 30 Junii.

Rot. Franciæ de anno 34 Edw. III. m. 6. De ſalva gardia pro abbate de Voto

CHERBOURG.   DIOCESE OF COUTANCE.

Voto juxta Cæsaris-burgum in Normannia. Ibid. pro abbate de Voto de restitutione Prioratus de Hagh. Teste rege apud Westminster. 22 Julii.

DIOCESE OF ROUEN.
(Continued from Vol. I. p. 62.)

FONTANELLA seu WANDREGISILIUS.

FONTENELLE, or ST. VANDRILLE.

A Benedictine abbey, six or seven leagues from Rouen, founded A. D. 654, by St. Wandregisilius, or, as the Monasticon says, by Richard the Second duke of Normandy. Soon after its foundation it had 500 monks, tho' now there are not above 20. It is at present known by the name of St. Vandrille.

The church was burnt 756, and again by the Normans 862, and not entirely rebuilt till 1033. The nave remains unfinished, and a beautiful centre,

centre tower, built 1331, fell down 1631, for want of repair, and deſtroyed two-thirds of the choir, the nave, S. tranſept, and our Lady's chapel. The religious of St. Maur, who were ſoon after introduced, rebuilt the whole. The fine collection of MSS. here was carried off and ſold 1580 by the ſacriſtan, and bought by Bigot and Ducheſne.

Deſcr. de la haute Norm. I. 78—85.

Monaſticon, tom. II. p. 949. 40. 104. a. b.

Neuſtria Pia, p. 131.

This houſe held the churches of Bridton, (Burton Bradſtock) Bridport and Whitchurch Canonicorum, in Dorſet, at the time of the Conqueror's ſurvey. Dorſetſhire Domeſday, tit. IX.

Hutchins

Hutchins I. 238. 324. 331. 343. A manor in Bincombe, in the same county. Ib. 339.

The church of Uphaven in Wiltshire being given to this abbey as early probably as the time of king Henry I. or that of king Stephen, a cell of Benedictine monks from thence was placed here. Tanner's Notitia, p. 598.

At Ecclesfield, in Yorkshire, was an alien priory of Benedictine monks belonging to this abbey. Ib. p. 683.

Rot. Pat. Normann. de anno 7 Hen. V. pars 2. m. 8. & 7. De confirmatione cartarum pro abbatia Sti. Wandragesilii de Rouen.

Rot. Normann. de anno 6 H. V. pars 2. m. 26. De restitutione temporalium

poralium abbati et conventui monafterii Sancti Wandragefilii.

FLORIACUM.

FLEURY.

A Benedictine abbey, founded A. D. 702, by Pepin de Heriftal, maire du palais to Childebert II. and fubject to St. Wandregefil.

Defcr. de la haute Norm. II. 271.
Neuftria Pia, p. 369.

CORNEVILLA.
CORNEVILLE.

At this place on the river Rile, two leagues from Pontaudemer, is a monastery, which was at first a priory, founded by Gilbert de Corneville, A. D. 1143, but was afterwards turned into an abbey of regular canons of St. Austin.

This abbey has never been considerable. It was totally destroyed by lightning, with all its buildings and furniture, 1287, but recovered itself by royal bounty. The religious of St. Maur, introduced into it 1659, have entirely rebuilt it. Descr. de la haute Normand. II. p. 319.

The annual income is 5000 livres, and it has the patronage of six churches. Neustria Pia, p. 877.

S. MARIA DE PRATIS.
PRATUM.

NOTRE DAME DE BONNES NOUVELLES AT ROUEN.

A Benedictine abbey founded A. D. 1063, on lands belonging to Bec abbey, by Queen Matilda, wife of William the Conqueror, and so called, because, according to tradition, she was here when she received the news of her husband's victory in 1066.

It was finished by Henry I. The whole, except the dormitory, was consumed by fire 1243, and the greatest part of the church by lightning 1351. The Hugonots committed great ravages in it in 1562, and at the siege of Rouen by Henry IV. of France,

France, 1591, it was burnt with the suburbs to save the city. It was rebuilt in its present form, between 1624 and 1655.

Hoveden says, the Empress Matilda, mother of Henry I. who died in 1166, was buried in the church of this abbey, where formerly was this epitaph:

> Ortu magna, viro major, sed maxima partu,
> Hic jacet Henrici filia, sponsa, parens.

But the monks of Bec claim her body for their church, where the English stript her tomb 1421, and where her remains were found 1684. See Hist. of Bec abbey, p. 98, 99.

Arthur I. duke of Bretagne, who died at Rouen 1203, was buried here, and many of the antient earls of Varenne,

renne, whose bones are lost in the ruins of the antient monastery. Descr. de la haute Norm. II. 47.

Monast. Angl. tom. II. p. 995.

Neustria Pia, p. 611.

Hist. de Rouen, tom. V. p. 450.

Rot. Normanni de anno 8 Hen. V. pars 1. m. 13.

De confirmatione pro priore & conventu de Prato.

COENOBIUM S. TRINITATIS IN MONTE.

MONASTERE DE LA SAINTE TRINITE' DU MONT A ROUEN.

This Benedictine abbey, which stood upon St. Catharine's hill, near Rouen, was founded, A. D. 1030, by Gosselin, Viscount d'Arques & de Dieppe, who

who became its first abbat. Afterwards, a castle being built here, this abbey was suppressed, and its estates given to the Chartreuse, near Gaillon, together with the several patronages formerly belonging to it.

 Monast. Angl. tom. II. p. 949. 52.
 Descr. de la haute Norm. II. 67.
 Hist. de la Ville de Rouen, tom. V. p. 336, & seq.

 At Harmondsworth, in Middlesex, was an alien priory of Benedictine monks, cell to the abbey of the Holy Trinity on the hill of St. Catharine, near Rouen. Tanner's Notitia, p. 312.

 At Blyth, in Nottinghamshire, was a priory of Benedictine Monks, built by Roger de Builly, and Muriel his wife, about A. D. 1088, to the honour

nour of the Blessed Virgin. It was in some respects subordinate to the abbey of the Holy Trinity in Monte St. Catherine, near Rouen. It was not seized, however, among the alien priories, but continued till the general dissolution. Ib. p. 400.

For their lands here, see Dr. Ducarel's Norman Antiquities, p. 39.

Rot. Norman. de anno 7 H. V. pars.... m. 46. De restitutione temporalium pro abbate et conventu Sanctæ Trinitatis in Monte Sanctæ Katherinæ prope Rothomagum.

Rymer's Fœdera, tom. VII. p. 697. Pro religiosis alienigenis, de licentia alienandi. Pat. 14 R. II. p. 2. m. 32. Teste R. ap. Westm. 10 Martii. Ubi recitatur concessio regis abbati monasterii

sterii S. Trinitatis in Monte S. Katerinæ juxta Rothomagum et conventui ejusdem loci, quod ipsi dare possint, concedere, et assignare venerabili in Christo patri Will. de Wykeham episcopo Winton. heredibus et assignatis suis imperpetuum maneria de *Hermondesworth* in com. Midd. et *Tyngewyk* in com. Buks. cum pertinent. ac omnia alia ad prædictos abb. & convent. & eorum pertinentia infra regnum nostrum Angliæ, præter prioratum de Blithe, cum pertinentiis.

GAILLE-FONTAINE.   DIOCESE OF ROUEN.

GOISLENIFONS.

GAILLE-FONTAINE.

A town in the Païs de Bray, where was an abbey of nuns, founded by Hugh de Gornay, about 1050.
Monasticon Angl. tom. II. p. 979. a. Descr. de la haute Norm. II. 117.

HOSPITALE LEPROSARUM DE KENILLI JUXTA ROTHOMAGUM.

PRIEURE' DU MONT AUX MALADES A ROUEN.

The inhabitans of Rouen, A. D. 1131, built a church dedicated to St. James, and an hospital for lepers, at this place, where there is a priory of monks of the order of St. Austin, to which

which Henry the first and second, Kings of England, have been benefactors. The monastic apartments were rebuilt 1664.

 Monast. Angl. tom. II. p. 1013. b.
Descr. de la haute Norm. II. 57.
Hist. de Rouen, tom. vi. p. 75.

GRANDIMONS.

PRIORE DE NOTRE DAME DU PARC DIT GRANDMONT LEZ ROUEN.

Henry II. King of England and Duke of Normandy, having given some lands in the forest of Rouvray to the monks of the order of Grandmont, they began to settle there in 1156; but finding themselves disturbed in their devotions by hunters, they applied

applied to this King, who gave them his park, and other lands near Rouen, where their Priory is at prefent (for which reafon their church is called Notre Dame du Parc), and confirmed the fame by his letters patent, dated July 3, anno regni 2, which fee at length in Hiftoire de la Ville de Rouen, vol. vi. p. 98. where, at p. 103, is the epitaph of Geoffry (Plantagenet) archbifhop of York, bafe fon to King Henry II. who died 1212, and lies buried in the church of this convent.

This priory having been a long time held in commendam, was united by Henry IV. to the Jefuits college.

The church was ruined about the end of the 14th century, and soon after its restoration was burnt down. The monastery did not recover the havock made in it by the league till 1652. Descr. de la haute Norm. II. 59.

See Rot. Normann. de anno 7 Hen. V. pars. 1. m. 26. De temporalibus restitutis Prioratui Beatæ Mariæ de Parc-lez-Rouen.

S. GEORGE DE BOCHERVILLE.   DIOCESE OF ROUEN.

COENOBIUM S. GEORGII BANQUERVILLÆ.
ST. GEORGE DE BOCHERVILLE.

A Benedictine abbey in the parish of Bocherville, two leagues from Rouen, near the river Seine; founded A. D. 1114, by Radulfus lord of Tancarville.

Its church, which was built about 1066, is of a massive stile, calculated to resist the violent winds which are frequent in this valley. It is 206 feet by 60 and 50 high; the transepts 96 by 26: both of them terminating like the choir, in a semicircle. The steeple is 180 feet high, and two slender towers rise over the W. door. The founder and his family are buried here. His 5th son William turned out the canons,

canons, and substituted monks of St. Evroul. The dormitory was rebuilt 1690.

Genetai, a country house just by this abbey, is remarkable for its artificial echo. Descr. de la haute Norm. II. 294.

Its annual income is 17000 livres, and the patronage of twenty churches.

Neustria Pia, p, 691.

Monast. Angl. tom. II. p. 954. a.

At Edith Weston, or Edyweston, in Rutlandshire, was an alien priory of Benedictine monks, cell to this abbey, to which it was given by William de Tankervill, chamberlain to king Henry I. Tanner's Notitia, p. 443.

S. GEORGE DE BOCHERVILLE.   **DIOCESE OF ROUEN.**

The said William de Tankervill, temp. Hen. I. gave the manor of Avebury in Wiltshire to this abbey; and so it became an alien priory to it. Ib. p. 597.

Rot. Normann. de anno 6 H. V. pars 2. m. 27. De restitutione temporalium abbati et conventui Sancti Georgii de Basquervilla.

Rot. Franc. 13 H. IV. m. 15. Pro monachis de Normannia.

BELLENCUMBRIS.

BELLENCOMBRE.

A Priory of the order of St. Auſtin, in a town of that name on the river Arques, in the Païs de Caux, founded by the lords de la Heuze; but at what time I have not been able to diſcover. Here ſeem to have been two diſtinct priories, afterwards united in one. At preſent there are no monks here. The king nominates the prior.

It is not taken notice of in Neuſtria Pia.

See Monaſt. Angl. tom. II. p. 1012. a.
Deſcr. de la haute Norm. I. p. 170.

S. MARTINUS DE ALCEIO.
ST. MARTIN D'ACY.

St. Martin d'Acy, near Albemarle or Aumale, in the diocese of Rouen, is a Benedictine abbey founded about A. D. 1030, by the lords of Aumale, and by the countess Adelize, who gave it to the monks of St. Lucien, of Beauvais, as we learn by Stephen earl of Aumale, her son, who confirmed this foundation by his letters, dated A. D. 1115. The income of the abbot is about 9000 livres.

It was ruined 1393. The church was rebuilt about the middle of the following century, and again with the whole house 1705--1729. In the vaults are buried many lords of Guise and Nemours. Descr. de la haute Norm. I. 59.

Stephen earl of Albemarle gave, A. D. 1115, to the Benedictine Monks of St. Martin de Alceio, near Albemarle, in Normandy, several tithes and churches in the East Riding of Yorkshire, and in the north part of Lincolnshire, who thereupon sent over a procurator or prior, with some monks of their own house, to look after the same. These, after some time, fixed their cell and continued in the chapel of St. Helen (at Burstall Garth, olim Birstall, in the deanry of Holderness, and archdeaconry of East Riding in Yorkshire) till the frequent seizing of the estates of the foreign abbies, during the wars with France, occasioned this alien priory to be sold

to

to the abbat and convent of Kirkſtall, 18 Ric. II. Tanner's Notitia, p. 647.

S. view of Burſtall, by Buck, 1721.

At Wythernefs, in Yorkſhire, a priory fubordinate to this abbey, is mentioned in the records in the reign of King John. Ib. p. 682.

MONASTERE DE LA ROSE DE NOTRE DAME.

COENOBIUM ROSÆ B. M.

This was the firſt monaſtery of Carthuſians at Rouen, founded A.D. 1384, by William de Leſtranges, archbiſhop of Rouen, but in 1682 united to the monaſtery of Carthuſians of St. Julien there, and totally deſtroyed 1702.

Deſcr. de la haute Norm. II. 67.

Pat.

Pat. Normann. de anno 6 H. V. pars 2. m. 39. De salva gardia pro priore & conventu domus Rosæ Beatæ Mariæ juxta Rothomagum & hominibus suis.

Rot. Normann. de anno 7 H. V. pars 1. m. 25. De salva gardia pro priore domus Rosæ Beatæ Mariæ juxta Rothomagum.

S. LAUDUS.
ST. LO.

A priory of regular canons of St. Austin, in the city of Rouen, founded A. D. 1144, by Algar bishop of Coutances, who have several privileges. The church belonging to this convent was formerly a cathedral, where Thierri, bishop of Coutances, fixed

fixed a fee. Different parts were rebuilt in 1362, 1455 and 1479.

Defcr. de la haute Norm. II. 52.

NOVIONUM AD ANDELLAM, or CAROLI VALLIS.

CHARLEVAL, antiently NOYON SUR ANDELLE.

Charleval is a town fo called ever fince Charles IX. king of France, built a caftle in this place; its antient name being Noyon fur Andelle. Here is a priory of Benedictine monks, founded A. D. 1107, by William earl of Evreux, whofe prior is nominated by the prior of St. Evrou, Ebrulfus, or Utica, to whom as well as the priory de Novo Mercato, in Normandy, it is fubordinate. That great houfe had eftates in feveral parts of England, but

but chiefly in Berkshire, where the prior of Noyon, or Nowne, as some of the records call it, had manors and lands to a good value, at East Henred, Henny, &c. some, or all of which, were given by Henry V. to his new-erected monastery at Sheen. Tanner's Notitia, p. 23.

NOVUS-MERCATUS.

NEUMARCHE.

Neumarche, a small town, where is a priory of Benedictine monks, whose prior is nominated by the prior of St. Ebrulfus.

DOMUS MONIALIUM ORD. S. DOMINICI JUXTA ROTHOMAGUM.

LE MONASTERE DES RELIGIEUSES DE ST. DOMINIQUE, DITES LES EMMURÉES.

Near the city of Rouen is a houſe of Nuns of the order of St. Dominic, called *les Emmurées, i. e.* locked up, becauſe theſe nuns never come out of this convent (which is ſurrounded with high walls) after they are once admitted into it. It was founded by St. Lewis, king of France, A. D. 1269. It ſuffered much in 1384 and 1418, and was twice entirely deſtroyed: once by the Proteſtants who took this city in 1562, and a ſecond time by the troops of the League in 1591. Notwithſtanding which it is remarkable, that the choir of the church remains entire as when firſt built by the founder. The reſt of the church was rebuilt 1608 and 1666.

Monaſt. Angl. tom. II. p. 1016. b.
Deſcript. de la haute Norm. II. 64.
Hiſt. de la ville de Rouen, tom. VI. p. 231. Rouen, 1738. 12mo.

North View of the Cathedral Church of EVREUX in Normandy

DIOCESE OF EVREUX.

(Continued from vol. I. p. 80.)

GRANDIMONS.

GRANDMONT.

A priory near the foreſt of Beaumont-le-Roger.

Monaſt. Angl. tom. ii. p. 979. b.

On the borders of Brecknockſhire, among the mountains in Ewyas land, was a monaſtery for a prior and ten religious, of the order of Grandmont in Normandy, ſettled at Creſſwell, Carefwell, or Keſſewell, in Herefordſhire, about the latter end of the reign of king John, or the beginning of king Henry III. probably by Walter Lacy. Tanner's Notitia, p. 177.

In the beginning of the time of king John, Joan, daughter of William Foſſard, wife to Robert de Turnham, gave a parcel of lands in the foreſt of Egheton, ſince called Erſkdale, (in Yorkſhire) to the abbot and convent of Grandmont in Normandy, who thereupon ſent a convent of monks, of their own order, to ſettle here; when, by reaſon of the wars with France, the kings of England bore hard upon theſe alien priories, the abbot of Grandmont got leave to ſell the advowſon, and all their right in this cell, to John Hewitt, alias Serjeaunt; and thereupon it ſeems to have become *prioratus indigena*, and to have ſubſiſted till the general diſſo-

dissolution, when there were not above four monks in it. Tanner's Notitia, p. 679.

Rot. Vasconiæ anni 13 E. I. m. 1. Pro priore grandis montis de fratribus ordinis sui inobedientibus capiendis. Dat. apud Westminster, 24 die Junii.

Rot. Normann. de anno 6 Hen. V. pars 2. m. 26. De restitutione temporalium priori & conventui de Grantmont.

S. SAUVEUR A EVREUX.

S. SALVATOR.

A Benedictine nunnery in the city of Evreux, founded A. D. 1055, by Richard earl of Evreux.

Monaſt. Angl. tom. II. p. 950. 29.

Rot. Normann. de anno 7 Hen. V. pars 1. m. 48. De ſalva gardia conceſſa abbatiſſæ & conventui Sancti Salvatoris de Evreux.

VERNON.   DIOCESE OF EVREUX.

VERNONUM, VERNUM, VEL VERNO.

VERNON.

A town situate upon the river Seine. The French kings had formerly a palace in this town; and St. Lewis, king of France, founded an hospital here in 1261.

See Monast. Angl. tom. II. p. 1014. a.

Rot. Normann. de anno 7 Hen. V. pars 1. m. 41. De havagio* villæ de Vernon cum pertinentiis, concesso hospitali de Vernon in perpetuam elemosinam.

See an account of it in Dr. Ducarel's Norman Antiq. p. 91, 92, &c.

* *Havagium* or *havadium*, *havage*, *havec*, a a tax paid for a certain measure of corn, or other dry goods. Du. Cange.

DIOCESE OF LISIEUX.
(Continued from vol. I. p. 100.)

LEXOVIENSIS.

LISIEUX.

A Benedictine nunnery in the city of Lisieux, founded A. D. 1050, by Lescelina countess of Eu, with the assistance of her sons, Robert earl of Eu, and Hugh bishop of Lisieux.

Monastic. Angliæ, tom. II. p. 950. 4.
Neustria Pia, p. 583.

North-West View of the
Cathedral of Bayeux, in Normandy.

DIOCESE OF BAYEUX.

(Continued from vol. I. p. 144.)

VILLARIUM,

VILLERS.

One of the 13 parishes in Normandy of the name of Villers, called Villers en Bocage, has an abbey of Benedictine nuns.

RADEVERUM.

RAVIERS.

A Benedictine abbey in the diocese of Bayeux, founded by St. Vigor, A. D. 545.

Neustria Pia, p. 65.

S. MARIA VILLARS.

VILLERS.

A Ciftertian nunnery, at a town now called Villers Canivet, founded A. D. 1140, by Roger de Mowbray*, poffeffed of lands at Wadone, [Friar's Waddon in Portifham.] Dorfetfhire Domefday, tit. 23. Hutchins I. 556. Neuftria Pia, p. 791.

* Mr. Hutchins fays, it was founded by St. Philibert for monks, and repaired for nuns by Judith, wife of Richard II. duke of Normandy. Mon. Angl. II. 949. 4. But quere, if this is not Montvilliers before mentioned.

LIBERIACUM.

LIVRAY, or LIOVRAY.

A small Benedictine abbey founded by St. Gerbold bishop of Bayeux, about A.D. 675.

DIOCESE OF AVRANCHES.

(Continued from vol. I. p. 157.)

BELLUS PORTUS.

BEAUPORT.

An abbey of Premonstratensians, in Britany, a cell to the abbey of La Luzerne, in the diocese of Avranches, founded by Alan earl of Goelo and Petronilla his wife, A. D. 1202.

Alan, son of Henry earl of Britany, gave, A. D. 1202, the town and church of West Ravendale, in Lincolnshire, to the Premonstratensian abbey of Beauport, in Britany, and so it became a cell to that monastery. It was valued at £14 per annum, and granted by Henry VI. to Southwell church. Tanner's Notitia, p. 278.

ADDENDA.

P. 14. CHERBOURG.

About half a mile from the town, is a cliff or rock of prodigious height, ascended by a long winding path across the adjoining mountains; and on its top a little convent of Benedictine monks or hermits, who there cultivate a few acres of barren stony ground. The superior shewed Mr. Wraxall the spot, now marked by a cross, from whence king John is said to have thrown his nephew Arthur into the sea, which now no longer washes the foot of this rock. W. of the town about a mile in a meadow on the river Chantereine is a small chapel, built by the Empress Matilda, who on her passage

passage to England, being overtaken by a violent storm, vowed to sing a hymn to the Virgin wherever she landed. This being the fortunate spot, one of the sailors reminded her of her vow, exclaiming, "Chante, reine, vechi terre," which gave name to the river. The chapel is in the rude style of the age, and ready to fall. In it is a box apparently coeval with it, and above on the wall an inscription almost effaced imploring contributions to it. See Wraxall's Tour, II. 189, &c.

ALIEN PRIORIES
IN OTHER PARTS OF
FRANCE.

DIOCESE OF AMIENS.

GEMELLENSE.

ST. MARTIN AUX JUMEAUX.

THE abbey of St. Martin aux Jumeaux is an abbey of regular canons of St. Auguſtine, in the city of Amiens, in Picardy, at firſt founded for a community of ſecular clerks, by Guy biſhop of Amiens, to whom the chapter of that cathedral gave conſiderable eſtates, A. D. 1073. Theſe clerks became afterwards regular canons of St. Auguſtine, A. D. 1109, and their community was turned into an abbey A. D. 1145.

De la Force, vol. III. p. 15.

FANUM SANCTI VALERICI.

ST. VALERY.

Saint Valery is a town ſituate at the mouth of the river Somme, four leagues below Abbeville, in the dioceſe of Amiens, where there is an abbey of Benedictine monks, founded by king Clothaire, A. D. 613, whoſe abbat enjoys an annual income of 13000, and the monks 9500 livres.

De la Force, vol. III. p. 20.

S. VALERY. DIOCESE OF AMIENS.

Takeley in Essex was an alien priory, cell to the abbey of St. Valery, in Picardy, to which the manor of Takeley was given by Henry I. Tanner's Notitia, p. 125.

Salmon's Essex, p. 100. Morant, in his account of the parish of Takely.

Monasticon, tom. II. p. 1003. a.

Rot. Fin. 31 E. III. m. 1.

DIOCESE OF ANGERS.

ANDEGAVUM.

ANGERS.

Angers is a bishop's see, and the capital of the province of Anjou.

Here is the Benedictine abbey of St. Nicholas, founded by Fulk de Nera, earl of Anjou.

The annual income of the abbat is 10 or 12,000 livres.

De la Force, Nouv. Descr. de la France, vol. VI. p. 162.

At Wileketone, Willoughton, or Wyllyton, in Lincolnshire, is said to have been an alien priory. Maud the empress did indeed give the church, or a moiety out of it, to the abbey of St. Nicholas

S. NICHOLAS.   DIOCESE OF ANGERS.

Nicholas by Angiers; and that abbey had a pension out of it; and a manor in Willoughton, lately belonging to that abbey, was granted by Henry VI. to King's college, Cambridge. But it is not certain there was a priory of monks here. Tanner's Notitia, p. 268.

At Kirkby or Monks-Kirby, in Warwickshire, was an alien priory of Benedictine monks, cell to this abbey, which owed its origin to the large grant of lands and tithes of this and other neighbouring towns, by Geoffrey de Winchia, or Wirce, A. D. 1077, to that foreign monastery. This cell, as well as the head house, was dedicated to St. Nicholas, and after many seizures during the wars with

with France, leave was given by the king, 20 Ric. II. to annex the same to the new-erected priory of Carthusians, in Axholm, near Epworth in Lincolnshire, upon which it was finally settled, 3 Hen. V. after it had been restored to the abbey of Angiers for some little time, during the reign of Henry IV. Henry VIII. granted it to Charles Brandon, duke of Suffolk, from whose family it past to the earl of Denbigh's, whose ancestors have monuments in the church; and the rectory to Trinity-college, Cambridge. Ib. 568. Dugdale's Warw. I. 75.

Yvo Tailbois, earl of Angiers, lord of Spalding, in the county of Lincoln, about the year 1074, gave the church of St. Mary, and the manor of Spalding,

Spalding, to the abbey of St. Nicholas at Angiers, from whence were sent over some Benedictine monks, and so it became an alien priory to that foreign monastery. It was naturalized by Edward IV. and at the dissolution granted to Sir John Cheke, being valued at £.767. 8s. 11d. per annum. A plan of it is in the Monasticon, but no remains at present, except part of the offices. Tanner's Notitia, p. 251.

Monasticon, tom. I. p. 306. 562. tom. II. p. 1000. a.

The church and other lands at Wenge, olim Guinuga*, in Buckinghamshire, being given by Maud the empress to the monastery of St. Ni-

* This seems the French orthography in the charters.

cholas

cholas at Angiers in France, a cell of Benedictine monks settled at a hamlet in this parish, since called Ascot. Ib. p. 26.

Pat. 4. H. V. part. 1. m. 20.
Monast. Angl. tom. II. p. 1000. a.

FONTEVRAULT.   DIOCESE OF ANGERS.

FONS EVRAUDI, vel EBRALDI.

FONTEVRAULT.

A celebrated abbey of Benedictine monks and nuns, in Anjou, a league from the Seine, founded A. D. 1100, by Robert de Arbrifcelle, for monks and nuns. The monks are governed by the abbefs, who is called Chef & Supericure Generale tant des Religieux que des Religieufes de cet Inftitut. See Longuerue, Defcription Hift. & Geographique de la France ancienne & moderne, fol. Paris 1722. p. 153.

Many convents in France are cells to this monaftery. Henry II. of England, was a great benefactor to it, and lies buried in the choir of its church,

church, with his wife Eleanor, his son Richard I. king of England, and Isabel de Angoulesme, 3d wife of John, king of England, his 3d son, who died a nun here. Their monuments are engraven in Sandford's Genealogical History of the Kings of England, p. 64. Rapin's History of England, vol. I. p. 242. fol. and in Monfaucon's Monumens de la Monarchie Françoise, tom. II. p. 114.

Monast. Anglic. tom. II. p. 948. 58. 975. a.

Rot. Vascon. de anno 1, 2, & 4 Edw. II. memb. 26. n. 7.

Pro abbatissa & monialibus de monasterio Fontis Ebraldi ad recipiendum arreragia centum et triginta librarum Turonensium annuarum pro insula de de Oleron. Data apud Westminster. 15 die Martii, anno 2 Ed. II.

Rot. Vascon. de annis 13 & 14 Ed. II. anno 14 Ed. II. m. 1. dorso. De solvendo redditus et arreragia in insula Oleronii abbatissæ et monialibus Fontis Ebroldi. Teste rege apud Westminster. 26 Maii.

At de la Grave, or Grove, now Grovebury, in the parish of Leighton in the county of Bedford, was an alien priory belonging to this abbey. See Tanner's Notitia, p. 6.

Robert Bossu earl of Leicester, founded temp. Hen. II. at Nun Eaton in Warwickshire, a priory for nuns of the order of Fontevrauld, wherein, besides the prioress and nuns, there was for some time a prior also,

perhaps

perhaps with men, as usually in the foreign houses of this order. Ib. p. 578.

Buck engraved an E. view of its ruins, 1729.

The abbess and nuns of Ambrosbury, in Wiltshire, being, A. D. 1177, expelled from thence for their ill lives, Henry II. placed herein a prioress and 24 nuns, from Font Ebrald, in Normandy, to which monastery this house was for some time subject, but at length was made denizon, and became again an abbey. Tanner's Notitia, p. 589.

Eustachia de Say and her son Osbert Fitz Hugh, having given the church of Westwood, near Droitwich in Worcestershire, and other lands there to the

the abbey of Fontevrauld in France, temp. Hen. II. here was shortly after a small priory, dedicated to the Blessed Virgin, for six nuns of the order of Fontevrauld. Ib. p. 624.

Cart. 9 E. I. m. 1. Pro monialibus de Ambresbir.

Edward I. in the 20th year of his reign, commanded the heart of his father Henry III. to be delivered to the abbess of Font-Evrauld, to be interred in that nunnery, according to his promise in his lifetime, which the abbat of Westminster accordingly delivered to her 20 years after his decease, in the presence of sundry bishops, nobles, and others, by the king's command. See Patent 20 E. I. m. 20. De corde

corde regis Henrici liberato abbatiſſæ Fontis Ebroldi ad ſepeliendum in monaſterio ſuo. Prynne's Life of King John, King Henry III. and King Edward I. p. 474.

Mary, ſixth daughter of Edward I. being a nun at Ambroſbury, the king granted her 40 oaks each year, 20 tun of wine, and ſeveral manors of above the value of £.200 a year for her maintenance, by patents, which ſee Pat. 30 E. I. m. 14. Pro Maria filia regis moniale de Ambreſbur. See Prynne's Life of King John, p. 937.

She was afterwards a nun at Font-Evraud. Sandford, p. 143.

Fontevrault.

The monuments of Henry II. Richard I. &c. at Fontevrault, are at present enclosed within the grate in that part of the church where the abbess and nuns assemble for public devotion; and no interest or intreaties can procure admittance into this sacred partition.—Four solemn requiem and services are said every year for the repose of the souls of these princes; and the church was repaired and beautified in 1638, by order of the abbess of Fontevrault. Besides its high antiquity it has ever been considered as one of the most honourable and important ecclesiastical benefices in France. Many princesses of the blood have successively governed it.

The revenues are immenfe. The number of religious of both fexes under the abbefs's direction amount to more than 200; and her authority both fpiritual and temporal is exceedingly extenfive. Ib. II. 400.

S. SERGIUS & S. BACHUS.

S. SIERGE ou S. SERGE D'ANGERS.

Called alſo in old writings St. Bachus, or St. Bach, and St. Medard, is a Benedictine abbey in the province of Anjou, founded, according to ſome authors, by Reomenus, prince of Britanny; others ſay, by Childebert, king of France. The annual income of the abbat is about 6500 livres.

De la Force, Nouvelle Deſcript. de la France, vol. VI. p. 162.

The church of St. Andrew at Swaveſey, in Cambridgeſhire, with the tithes thereunto belonging, being given temp. Will. Conq. by Alan Rufus, or la Zuſche, or Zouch earl of Britanny and Richmond, to the abbey

abbey of St. Sergius and Bachus, it became a cell of Benedictine monks to that foreign monastery. After that the alien priories during the wars with France were often seized, this was given, or rather sold, by the French abbat and convent, to the priory of St. Anne, near Coventry, by licence from king Richard II. and afterward confirmed by authority of parliament, 6 Hen. IV. Tanner's Notitia, p. 41.

Totness in Devonshire was an alien priory, cell to the abbey of St. Sergius and St. Bachus at Angiers, to which the church of St. Mary there, and several other lands, were given by Johel fil. Aluredi temp. Will. Conq. The monks here were of the Cluniac,

or

or Benedictine order, and were not dissolved temp. Hen. V. but continued till the general suppression, when it was valued at £.24. 9s. 2¼d. per ann. as Dugdale; or as Speed and Stevens, £.124. 10s. 2¼d. Ib. p. 89.

Truwardraith, Tuwardraz, or Tywardreit, in the deanry of Powder in Cornwall, was an alien priory of Benedictine monks, belonging to the abbey of St. Sergius and Bachus, in Angiers, founded before A. D. 1169, by Champernulphus or Chambernon, of Bere, lord of the manor of Tywardreith, or by the ancestors of Robert de Cardinan, perhaps Robert Fitz-William. Annual value at the suppression £.123. 9s. 3d. Ib. p. 70.

Minster, in the deanry of Trigg Minor, in Cornwall, was also an alien priory belonging to this abbey. Ibid. p. 71.

Monasticon, tom. I. p. 572.
Rot. Pip. 13 E. III.
Pat. 48 E. III. part. 2. m. 23.

S. FLORENTIUS.

S. FLORANT DE SAUMUR.

A Benedictine abbey in the province of Anjou, founded by the emperor Charlemagne, and rebuilt by Lewis le Debonnaire and Charles the Bald. This monastery was situate in a place at that time called *le Mont Glonna*, which was famous on account of the death of St. Florentinus.

rentinus. The Normans deftroyed it about A. D. 947, and drove the monks from thence. Thibaud earl of Tours, Blois, and Chartres, collected the remains of the community of St. Florant *le Vieux*, and built them a monaftery in the caftle of Saumur, A. D. 950. Fulk Nerra, earl of Anjou, having befieged and taken Saumur, deftroyed the abbey of St. Florant, and the monks were obliged to retire a quarter of a league from Saumur, where the abbey of St. Florant is at prefent, whofe abbat enjoys an annual income of about 20000 livres.

De la Force, vol. VI. p. 162.
Monafticon, tom. II. p. 973. a.
Pat. 2 R. II. part. 2. m. 24.

The church of St. Mary, at Andover, in Hampshire, with the appurtenances, viz. a hyde of land, several rents, &c. being given to the French abbey of St. Florence, at Salmur in Anjou, by king William the Conqueror, it became a cell to that monastery. Tanner's Notitia, p. 158.

Wihenoc de Monemue, or Monmouth, temp. Hen. I. brought over a convent of black monks from St. Florence, near Salmur in Anjou, and placed them first in the church of St. Cadoc, near the castle, and after in the church of St. Mary at Monmouth. It was made denison, and at the suppression valued at £.56. 1 s. 11 d. per annum. Ib. p. 26.

Sporle,

S. FLORANT.   DIOCESE OF ANGERS.

Sporle, in Norfolk, was an alien priory of black monks belonging to the abbey of St. Florence, near Salmur. Mr. Blomefield afcribes its foundation to Henry II. who was earl of Anjou, and in whofe reign it exifted. Hift. of Norf. III. 443. It was given to Eton college by Henry VI. Tanner's Notitia, p. 358.

William de Braiofa having, A. D. 1075, given to the abbey of St. Florence at Salmur, the churches of St. Peter at Sele, St. Nicholas at Bramber, St. Nicholas at Shoreham, and fome others in Suffex, there was foon after fixed a convent of Benedictine monks from that foreign monaftery, which was made denizon 19 R. II. valued at £.29. 9s. 9d. per annum, and

and to St. Mary Magdalen college, Oxford. Ib. p. 552.

Monasticon, tom. I. p. 552. 580. 600.

ST. MAURICE D'ANGERS.

See a confirmation from Henry II. to the bishop and canons of St. Maurice of Anjou, of the donations made to them by Henry I. with divers franchises and immunities. Mad. Formulare, No. LXXXV.

The west end of the cathedral church of St. Maurice was published some years since " à Paris, chez " Jacques Chereau, Rue St. Jacques, " au grand St. Remy. Avec Privilege " du Roy."

DIOCESE OF BEAUVAIS.

S. LUCIANUS.

ST. LUCIEN.

Beauvais is a city, and a bishop's see, in the isle of France, where is a magnificent Benedictine abbey, called St. Lucien-lez-Beauvais, where the monks pretend they have the body of that saint.

De la Force, vol. II. p. 437.

At Wedon Pinkney, in the county of Northampton, was a Benedictine priory, dedicated to St. Mary, founded by Gilo de Wedon, lord here, and cell to St. Lucian, near Beauvais, as early probably as the reign of Henry I.

It was liberally endowed by several of the Pinkenies, who were lords here. But the wars between England and France hindering the monks of St. Lucian from enjoying the revenues of it, they sold their right, A. D. 1392, to the abbat and convent of Bittlesden, in Buckinghamshire, who enjoyed it not long, for about A. D. 1440, it was made part of the endowment of All Souls college in Oxon, Tanner's Notitia, p. 378.

Monasticon, tom. I. p. 584.

Bridges's Northamptonshire, I. 256.

DIOCESE OF BOURDEAUX.

ABBATIA SILVÆ MAJORIS.

ABBAYE DE LA SEAUVE MAJEUR.

This is an abbey of Benedictine monks in the city of Bourdeaux, founded by St. Gerard, difciple of St. Arnoul, bifhop of Soiffons, A. D. 1077, and dedicated to the Virgin Mary.

De la Force, vol. IV. p. 223.

At Burwell in Lincolnfhire was an alien priory of Benedictine monks, given by fome of the lords of Kyme to the abbey of St. Mary Silvæ Majoris, near Bourdeaux. Tanner's Notitia, p. 281.

Monafticon, tom. I. p. 579.

Rot.

Rot. Vasconiæ de anno 19 Hen. VI. memb. 2. De confirmatione pro abbate monasterii et conventu ecclesiæ B. M. de Silva Majore de libertatibus suis et aliis concessis per cartas Alienoræ reginæ, et Ricardi primi regis Angliæ. Teste Rege apud Westminster. 28 die Junii.

Rot. Vasconiæ de anno 14 E. II. m. 8. dorso. De defendendo abbatem Silvæ Majoris super mercato et jurisdictione ibidem. Teste Rege apud Haddeley, 26 Julii.

DIOCESE OF CHALONS.

CISTERTIUM.

CISTEAUX.

The abbey of Cisteaux, or Cîteaux, is a magnificent house, chief of the order of Cistertians, first established here 1098, situated in the diocese of Châlons, in the province of Burgundy. It was built by Eudo duke of Burgundy, A. D. 1068, and has several considerable privileges. The abbat is *Consiliarius natus* in the parliament of Burgundy, superior general of his order, and of five orders of knighthood which belong to it in the kingdoms of Spain and Portugal.

De la Force, vol. III. p. 253.

The church of St. Mary, and some lands at Scarborough in Yorkshire, being given to the abbat and convent of Ciftertium in France, some monks from that house and order were sent over, and had a cell here before the fourth year of king John, given at the suppression to Bridlington priory. Tanner's Notitia, p. 681.

DIOCESE OF CHARTRES.

S. NICASIUS MELLENTI.

ST. NICAISE DE MEULANT.

Meulant is a town situated upon the river Seine, eight leagues below Paris, having a bridge over the Seine, and a conventual priory of Benedictines, dedicated to Saint Nicaise, founded A. D. 670.

Neustria Pia, p. 331.

Frontispiece du grand portail de l'Eglise cathedrale de Notre Dame a Chartres; à Paris, chez Jacque Chereau.

TIRONIUM.
TIRON.

Tiron is a town situate two leagues from Nogent-le-Rotrou, in the province of Orleannois, where there is a Benedictine abbey, founded A. D. 1109, by Bernard de Abbeville, companion to Robert de Arbriſſel (founder of the abbey of Font-Evraud). This Bernard was the firſt abbat, and his ſucceſſors enjoy an annual income of about 4000 livres.

The order of St. Maur was introduced here, 1629.

De la Force, vol. X. p. 144.

Hamele, or Hamelriſe, in Hampſhire, was an alien priory of Ciſtertian monks, cell to the abbey of Tirone

rone in France, dedicated to St. Andrew. Thefe monks were fettled here in the time of Henry Blois, bifhop of Winchefter. Tanner's Notitia, p. 178.

Monafticon, tom. II. 958. 40.
See Rot. Pip. 13 E. III.

DIOCESE OF DOL.

S. JACUTUS.

ST. JACUT, or JAGU.

A Benedictine abbey built in the fifth century, in the province of Britanny.

De la Force, vol. VIII. p. 188.

The church of Lynton in Cambridgeshire, is said to have been given to the abbey of St. Jacutus de Insula, in the diocese of Dole in Britanny, by an earl of Britanny. An alien priory subordinate to this abbey occurs temp. Hen. III. Tanner's Notitia, p. 48.

Vid. Inquis. gen. com. Cantab. temp. Ed. I.

THE ALIEN PRIORIES.

S. JACUT.   DIOCESE OF DOL.

At Ifelham in Cambridgeshire, was a priory dedicated to St. Margaret, and cell to this abbey. Tanner's Notitia, p. 50.

Pat. 33 E. III. pars 2. m. 2.

DIOCESE OF LANGRES.

CLARAVALLIS.

CLAIRVAUX.

An abbey of Benedictine monks, in a small town of its name on the river Aube, in the province of Champagne, of which the celebrated St. Bernard was first abbat, 1116, founded by Hugo earl of Troyes the year before, and afterwards enriched by Theobald earl of Champagne, and by the earls of Flanders, more especially by Philip and Matilda his wife. The annual income is about 60000 livres.

Its church is large and fine, but not much adorned.

De la Force, vol. III. p. 82.

CLAIRVAUX. DIOCESE OF LANGRES.

William de Ipre, earl of Kent, who afterwards became monk at Laon in France) founded at Boxley in Kent, A. D. 1146, an abbey of Ciftertian monks, from Claravelle in Burgundy, (Tanner's Notitia, p. 213.) Its church was famous for a rood, which was contrived to move its eyes, hands and feet, till the impofture was detected by Cromwell and Cranmer, and the figure publicly burnt.

DIOCESE OF LIMOGES.

GRANDMONT LIMOUSIN.

The abbey of Grandmont, situate in the Haute Marche, in the province of Limousin, is the chief or head abbey of an order of that name. This order, which varied somewhat from that of St. Benedict, was instituted about A. D. 1076, by St. Stephen de Thiern, or Tiers, a gentleman of Auvergne, surnamed de Muret, because it was on a mountain of that name that he first settled this convent, which after his death was translated to Grandmont by his monks. This order was governed by priors till A. D. 1318, when William Belliceri was appointed abbat.

The

GRANDMONT.   DIOCESE OF LIMOGES.

The church and convent built by Henry I. and II. and Richard I. king of England, are entirely ruined, and were not rebuilt in La Force's time, but the society resided in a small building lately erected, the abbat general having no fund but his savings to build with.

De la Force, vol. XI. p. 381.

Warine, sheriff of Shropshire, and a great warrior against the Welsh, founded near Alberbury, or Abberbury, in Shropshire, the new abbey for Black monks of the order of Grandmont Limosin, temp. Hen. I. when they were first brought into England. Tanner's Notitia, p. 449.

Dugdale's Monasticon, vol. I. p. 605.

The preface to bishop Tanner's Not. Mon. p. xv. makes Cresswell in Herefordshire, and Eskdale in Yorkshire, of this order, though in their respective articles, p. 177. 679. they are made cells to the abbey of Grandmont in *Normandy*. See before, p. 43, 44.

DIOCESE OF MANS.

PERSENIA.

PERSEIGNE.

A Ciftertian abbey belonging to Normandy, though in the diocefe of Mans, founded A. D. 1145, by William Talvas earl of Alençon, Seez, and Bellefme.

Neuftria Pia, p. 817.

S. KARILEFUS.

SAINT CARILEF, vulgo S. CALAIS.

This abbey of St. Carilef, vulgo St. Calais, is in the city of Mans, a bishop's fee, capital of the territory of Maine, which is the N. part of Orleanois. It is an abbey of Benedictine monks, originally founded, as it is supposed, by Saint Thuribe bishop of Mans. St. Carilef, alias S. Calais, having rebuilt this abbey at the end of the sixth century, it is now called by his name. The income of the monks is 9000 livres, and that of the abbat about 10000 livres.

De la Force, vol. V. p. 192.

Some lands at Covenham, in Lincolnshire, being given, about A. D. 1082,

1082, to the abbey of St. Karilefus, in the diocese of Mans, by William the Conqueror, at the instance of William [de Carilefo] bishop of Durham, there were settled a prior and Benedictine monks from that foreign monastery, to which it continued a cell under the patronage of the bishops of Durham, till it was made over, 31 Ed. I. to the abbat and convent of Kirkstede, in whom it continued till the dissolution. Tanner's Notitia, p. 252.

Monasticon, tom. I. p. 555.

MONASTERIUM S. VINCENTII IN CENEMONIA.

S. VINCENT.

This is an abbey of Benedictine monks, situate in the suburbs of the city of Mans, founded in the sixth century, by St. Domnolus, bishop of Mans. The annual income of the abbat is about 36000 livres.

De la Force, vol. V. p. 191.

Hamelin Balon, or Baladun, one of those who came over with the Conqueror, founded in the latter end of his reign, or the beginning of William Rufus, a priory at Bergavenny, or Abergavenny, in Monmouthshire, to the honour of the Blessed Virgin. One of his posterity, William de Breosa,

t. John, gave the tithes of the castle, and other privileges, on condition that the abbat of St. Vincent, at Mans, would send over hither a convent of their Benedictine monks. So it seems to have been for some time an alien priory, cell to that foreign house, and continued till the dissolution, when it was valued at £.129. 5s. 8d. per annum. Tanner's Notitia, p. 328.

Monasticon, tom. I. p. 556.

DIOCESE OF MASCON.

CLUNIACUM.

CLUGNY.

Clugny is a town situate upon the river Gosne, in the province of Burgundy. It is famous for its abbey, which is the chief or head abbey of the order of Clugny, instituted A. D. 912, by Odo abbat of this abbey, which was founded A. D. 910, by William the first, duke of Aquitaine and Auvergne, on his own fee. Its church is the largest in France, being 620 feet in length, and 120 in width. The annual income of the abbat is 40000, and that of the monks about 60000 livres.

CLUGNY. DIOCESE OF MASCON.

De la Force, vol. IV. p. 157 and 335.

This church was built by Saint Hugh, and confecrated by Pope Innocent II. and has double tranfepts, the upper of which is 200 feet long, the lower 120. A great number of eminent perfonages have been buried in it. Cardinal Bouillon had erected a fumptuous maufoleum for himfelf, but, on his quitting France againft the king's orders, the king caufed it to be demolifhed. The treafury was one of the richeft in the kingdom, before it was thrice plundered by the Calvinifts, who are faid to have got above two millions the laft time. The library was full of MSS. An old catalogue makes their number 1800. Ib.

William the Conqueror is said to have first founded a monastery at Mons Acutus, or Montacute, in Somersetshire; but William earl of Moreton seems to have more amply endowed it, and granted it to the monks of Clugny, in the beginning of the reign of Henry I. Tanner's Notitia, p. 467.

In the beginning of the reign of king Henry I. William Peverell built a priory at Lenton in Nottinghamshire to the honour of the Holy Trinity, and made it subject to the great foreign abbey of Clugny. Ib. p. 402.

At St. Helen's, in the Isle of Wight, was a priory of Cluniac monks, before A. D. 1155, who being aliens, their revenues were seized

seized by king Edward II. and III. during their wats with France, but restored by Henry IV. Ib. p. 163.

Mr. Stow says, that there was one hospital in St. Andrew's, Holbourn, another in the street without Aldersgate, and another near Cripplegate, cells to the house of Clugny in France, which were suppressed 3 Hen. V. among the priories alien. If there were such, probably they were founded before the reign of king Edward III. whose seizures of all estates belonging to the French abbies discouraged all foundations of that kind. Ib. p. 319.

Monasticon, tom. II. p. 1006. b.

DIOCESE OF NEVERS.

PRIORATUS DE CARITATE.

LA CHARITÉ.

La Charité is a priory situate upon the river Loire, in the province of Nivernois, founded by a powerful lord named Roland, first at Seyr, about A. D. 700, for monks of St. Basil; destroyed by the Vandals 743; re-founded by king Pepin for Benedictines, and after a second destruction 755, by William II. earl of Nevers, &c. for Cluniacs. Its present name was given it on account of the charities given by the Cluniac monks of this rich priory, the prior whereof is lord spiritual and temporal of the town.

De la Force, vol. X. p. 386.

Roger of Montgomery, earl of Arundel, Chichester and Shrewsbury, endowed and built a monastery at Wenlock in Shropshire, 14 William the Conqueror, placing therein a prior and convent of Cluniac monks, who were looked upon as a cell to the house De Caritate in France. Tanner's Notitia, p. 444.

Of the beautiful ruins of Wenlok we have views by Buck, 1731. Grose, 1774. P. Sandby in the Virtuosi's Museum, 1778.

Aylwin Child, citizen of London, about the year 1082, began a new and fair church to the honour of our holy Saviour, with design to place therein a convent of monks of the Cluniac order,

order, who were procured from the priory De Caritate in France, by means of Archbifhop Lanfranc, A. D. 1089, about which time king William Rufus augmented the fmall eftate which Aylwin had procured for thefe religious, with the grant of the manor of Bermondfey, and other revenues. Tanner's Notitia, p. 535.

DIOCESE OF ST. OMERS.

S. BERTINUS.

ST. BERTIN.

St. Omers is a city of the French Netherlands, in the province of Artois, and the see of a bishop, where is the ancient and famous abbey, founded A. D. 626, by St. Bertinus, the companion of St. Omer, into which the Cluniacs were introduced, A. D. 1101. Its annual income is upwards of 100000 livres.

De la Force, vol. II. p. 91.

Thurlegh, Trewelegh, or Throuley, in Kent, was an alien priory of Cluniac monks, cell to this abbey. Tanner's Notitia, p. 222.

DIOCESE OF ORLEANS.

S. BENEDICT, supra LEYR.

ABBAYE DE FLEURY, ou DE SAINT BE-NOIT SUR LOIRE.

An abbey of Benedictine monks, founded about A. D. 623, by Leodebod, abbat of Saint-Aignan at Orleans. The income of the abbat is about 18000 livres per annum.

De la Force, vol. X. p. 138.

Ranulph de Meschines, earl of Chester, before the year 1129, gave the church of St. Andrew, at Minting in Lincolnshire, to this abbey, whereupon an alien priory of Benedictine monks was fixed here. Tanner's Notitia, p. 257.

Monasticon, tom. I. p. 592.

DIOCESE OF PARIS.

ABBATIA S. VICTORIS PARISIIS.

The ROYAL ABBEY of ST. VICTOR at PARIS.

Dugdale mentions this abbey as being first founded by William de Campellis, archdeacon of Paris, Mon. Angl. II. p. 948. 16. but Germain Brice, in his Defcription de la Ville de Paris, tom. II. p. 358. thinks it was first endowed by Louis le Gros, king of France, for regular canons, whom he settled there.

PRIORATUS S. MARTINI DE CAMPIS PARISIIS.

ST. MARTIN DES CHAMPS AT PARIS.

A very antient and rich priory of Cluniac monks, whofe income is above 45000 livres per annum.

At Barnftaple in Devonfhire was a cell to this abbey, which was afterwards made denifon, and continued till the general fuppreffion, when it was valued at £.123. 6s. 7d.. Tanner's Notitia, p. 90.

Baldwin de Redveriis, or Rivers, earl of Devonfhire, gave the chapel of St. James without Exeter, with the tithes and other eftates, to the head monaftery of St. Peter at Cluny, and to the abbey of St. Martin de Campis,

Campis, near Paris, before A. D. 1146, that a prior and some monks of that order might be settled here; which was accordingly done, and it became subordinate to this last mentioned house. After its suppression, Henry VI. gave its lands to King's college, Cambridge. Ib. p. 92.

A large view of Notre Dame* at Paris, by Anthony Aveline; Paris, no date.

Large plan of ditto; Paris, chez Jaubert.

Beautiful view of the altar-piece of ditto; Paris, chez Marriette.

View of the choir, the pictures, &c. by the same.

* This and the following plates are here enumerated as curiosities, though belonging to a different church.

Plan

Plan of the new pavement, by the fame.

Roman antiquities found under the altar of ditto, 1711. F. Delamonce del. G. Scotin major fculp. in a tract entitled " Obfervations fur les Monu-" mens d'Antiquité trouvez dans " l'Eglife Cathedrale de Paris. Par " M. Moreau de Mautour." 4to. Paris, 1711.

S. DIONYSIUS.

ST. DENYS.

An abbey of Benedictine monks not far from Paris, built and founded A. D. 639, by Dagobert king of France, and since that time much enriched by his successors. Many of the French kings are buried in the church belonging to this abbey.

Hist. de l'Abbaye Royale de St. Denys en France, par Dom. Michel Felibien, fol. Paris, 1706, with views of this abbey, and many prints.

South view of the church of St. Dennis. J. Marot fecit; à Paris, chez Pierre Marriette.

Edward the Confessor gave the monastery of Deerhurst in Gloucestershire,

shire, with all the lands belonging thereunto, to the abbey of St. Denys in France, to which it became a cell of Benedictine monks. It had eight lordships, and was accounted worth 300 marks by the year, when it was sold by the abbat and convent of St. Denys, to Richard earl of Cornwall, A. D. 1250. It was made denizon in the French wars of Henry VI.; but this denization was afterwards annulled, and that king granted it to Eton college, anno reg. 26. Edward IV. gave it successively to Foderinghay* and Eton colleges, and Tewkesbury abbey; and at the dissolution it was

* Foderinghay college was not suppressed till the reign of king Edward VI.

made private property. Tanner's Notitia, p. 140.

See also Domesday in Gloucestershire, Derheft hundred.

At Riddrefield, now Rotherfield, in Sussex, lands being given by Berthwald duke of the South Saxons, about the year 800, to the abbey of St. Denys in France, a convent of monks from that house were fixed here. Ib. p. 549. The church is dedicated to St. Dennis.

Monasticon, tom. I. p. 547. tom. II. p. 984. b.

This abbey had possessions at *Wilt* in Worcestershire; and at *Trigtone* in Oxfordshire. Domesday.

DIOCESE OF PERIGORD.

CASTELLIO.
CHASTILLON.

An abbey dedicated to St. Peter (order and founder unknown), fituated in the town of Chaftillon*, in the province of Guienne in Fronce, 16 miles eaft of Bourdeaux.

See grant of this abbey to the Ciftertian abbey of Bordefley in Worcefterfhire of tithes at Wotton and Langelega, dat. A. D. 1231. Madox's Formulare, No. DXXXVI.

---

* De la Force (VII. 297.) makes no mention of an abbey at *Caftillon* in Guienne; but at *Chaftillon*, in Burgundy, were feveral convents and an hofpital, dedicated to St. Peter. Ib. IV. 102.

THE ALIEN PRIORIES.

DIOCESE OF POITIERS.

MONASTERIUM NOVUM S. JOHANNIS PICTAVIÆ.

MONTIER-NEUF.

An abbey of Cluniac monks, in the city of Poitiers, the capital of the province of Poitou, and the see of a bishop. It was founded by Geoffrey earl of Poitiers, and duke of Aquitaine, A. D. 1068, and endowed by William VII. duke of Aquitaine his son, A. D. 1077. This is the only Cluniac monastery that has retained the title of abbey. Its annual income is 6000 livres.

De la Force, vol. VIII. p. 44.
Monasticon, tom. II. p. 991.

DIOCESE OF RENNES.

FULGERIÆ seu FILICERIÆ.

FOUGERES.

Fougeres is a town in Brittany, situate upon the river of Couesnon, on the borders of Normandy, where there is a priory of the order of St. Augustine, founded about A. D. 1163.

De la Force, vol. VIII. p. 282.

The manor of Ipelpen (in the deanry of Ipelpen, and archdeaconry of Totness) in Devonshire was given by the Conqueror to Ralph de Fulgeriis; and, by one of that family, the church and some lands here were given to the priory of St. Peter de Fulgeriis

Fulgeriis in Brittany; so it became a cell to that house. Tanner's Notitia, p. 93.

Monasticon, tom. II. p. 1012. b.

Rot. Pip. 13 E. III.

SANCTUS MELANIUS.

S. MELAINE.

St. Melaine at Rennes (the antient *Condate*, and called in modern Latin *Redones*) is an abbey of Benedictine monks, founded by Solomon II. A. D. 630, or 648, or by Paternus bishop of Avranches, in the province of Brittany.

De la Force, vol. VIII. p. 169.

Aubrey de Vere, the second of that name, father to the earl of Oxford, before A. D. 1140, gave the church of St. Mary at Hatfield Regis or Broadoke, in Essex, to the monks of St. Melanius at Redon in Brittany, upon which it probably became a cell to that foreign abbey. Tanner's Notitia, p. 127.

See his son the earl's confirmation charter in Salmon's Essex, p. 86. His son Robert was buried here, and his effigies cross-legged in stone still remains on the N. side of the altar. Dr. Hutton, in his collections from the London register, found that this church was dedicated to St. Mel*o*rius, quere, Mel*a*nius. Tanner's Notitia, ib.

DIOCESE OF RHEIMS.

S. REMIGIUS.

S. REMY at REIMS.

Rheims or Reims is the capital of the province of Champagne in France, one of the moſt elegant cities in that kingdom, and the ſee of an archbiſhop. In this city is the Benedictine abbey of St. Remy, founded about the middle of the ſixth century, whereof Turpin archbiſhop of Reims was the firſt abbat, about A. D. 770, and his ſucceſſors, till 945, filled both places. Its annual income is 32000 livres for the abbat, and 2000 for the monks.

The church was finiſhed A. D. 880, rebuilt 1018, its porch, towers, &c. 1162. South porch 1481. It is a large

large handsome building, but dark. Its beautiful Mosaic pavement full of scripture histories, &c. was made by a monk of this house in the thirteenth century. The tomb of St. Remy, erected 1531, contains his shrine and the Sainte Ampoule, or holy phial, containing the oil wherewith the kings of France are anointed. Most of the archbishops of Rheims before the eleventh century are buried here. The monastery is a spacious structure, and has a good library.

De la Force, vol. III. p. 207-216.

Lappele in Staffordshire was an alien priory of Black monks, from the abbey of St. Remigius at Rheims, to which it was given, temp. Ed. Conf. by Algar earl of Chester or Mercia.

Upon

Upon the frequent seisures of this estate into the king's hands during the wars with France, the foreign abbat and convent determined, about 4 Ric. II. to sell it to Thomas Cotterell, clerk, and his assigns. But this seems not to have taken effect, for this cell coming to the crown upon the general suppression of these kind of houses, was given by king Henry V. to Tong College in Shropshire, and so continued till the surrender of the same. Tanner's Notitia, p. 492.

Monasticon, tom. I. p. 1022. tom. II. p. 993. a.

It had possessions at *Mepford* and *Rideware* in Staffordshire; and in the hundred of *Ovret* in Shropshire. Domesday.

THE CATHEDRAL AT RHEIMS, though not known to be connected with England, being one of the moſt ſuperb ſtructures of the kind, deſerves to be mentioned for its beautiful W. front.

Le ſomptueux frontiſpice de l'Egliſe Notre Dame de Rheims, by Deeſon, 1625, prefixed to " Le deſſein de l'Hiſtoire de Reims. Par feu M. Nicolas Bergier. Reims, 1635." 4to.

The beautiful weſt end of the cathedral church of Notre Dame de Rheims, with the proceſſion of Louis XV. at his coronation, October 23, 1722. Paris, chez De Mortain.

Plan of this church and the archbiſhop's palace. Ibid.

DIOCESE OF TREGUIER.

BEGARDUM.

BEGARD, or BEGARS.

A Ciftertian abbey in the province of Britanny, founded A. D. 1135, by Stephen the Third, earl of Penthievre and Evoifa de Guingam his wife.

De la Force, vol. VIII. p. 183.

The abbey of Begare in Britanny having feveral eftates in England, particularly in Lincolnfhire and Yorkfhire, there was a cell of alien monks of that abbey fixed at Begare, near Richmond in the county of York, temp. Hen. III. granted at the fuppreffion preſſion ſucceſſively to the chantry of St. Anne at Threſk, then to Eaton college, then to the priory of Mountgrace, and at laſt to Eaton college again. Tanner's Notitia, p. 683.

DIOCESE OF TOURS.

MAJUS MONASTERIUM.

MARMOUTIER.

A Benedictine abbey in the suburbs of Tours, founded by St. Martin, and being the most considerable of the three monasteries founded by him, is for that reason called Majus Monasterium. It was destroyed by the Normans 853, restored for canons, and after for Benedictines. Its revenue is 18000 livres, and that of its abbot 16000. It has been united to the archbishopric of Tours.

De la Force, vol. XI. p. 25. 49.

Tykeford,

Tykeford, or Tickford, near Newport Pagnell in Buckinghamshire, was a cell of Cluniac monks subordinate to this abbey, to which this manor was given by Fulk Painel, in the reign of William Rufus. It was subjected by Henry IV. to the other cell of the Holy Trinity at York, and was dissolved for Cardinal Wolsey, being valued at £.126. 17*s*. per ann. Tanner's Notitia, p. 24.

Trinity, or Christ Church, in the west part of the city of York, was a church dedicated to the Holy Trinity, in which were formerly canons endowed with lands, but these being dispersed, and their house almost ruined, Ralph Painell, by the favour of William the Conqueror, got possession

session of it, and A. D. 1089, gave it to the Benedictine monks of St. Martin Marmoutier at Tours in France, who made it a cell to their abbey. It was made denizon by Henry VI. and valued at the dissolution at £. 109. 9 *s*. 10 *d*. per annum. Ibid. p. 641. Drake's York, p. 263.

Allerton Malleverer, in the deanry of Boroughbridge, and archdeaconry of Richmond, in Yorkshire, was an alien priory to this abbey, to which the church of St. Martin there, was given by Richard Malleverer, and confirmed to them by king Henry II. At the dissolution of foreign cells, Henry VI. gave it to King's college, Cambridge. Ib. p. 672.

Monasticon, tom. I. p. 563. 599. 685. tom. II. p. 991. a.

Pat. 46 E. III. pars 2. m. 45.

Burton's Monast. Ebor. p. 258.

SEE a fine west view of the Metropolitan Church of ST. GRATIEN AT TOURS, engraved by Jacques Cherreau at Paris, no date.

DIOCESE OF VIENNE.

VIENNA.

VIENNE.

Vienne, in the province of Dauphiné, is the see of an archbishop, and has an abbey of monks of the order of St. Augustine, dedicated to St. Anthony, which is the chief or head of that order.

It was at first an hospital, but was turned into an abbey by Pope Boniface VIII. Its annual income is about 40000 livres per annum.

De la Force, vol. IV. p. 53.

On the north side of Threadneedle-street, in the parish of St. Bennet Fink, was a synagogue of the Jews, A. D. 1231,

1231, which was given by Henry III. to the brethren of St. Anthony of Vienne in France, who settled herein an hospital, consisting of a master, two priests, a school-master, and twelve poor brethren, besides their proctors and other officers and servants. Tanner's Notitia, p. 314.

DIOCESE OF GHENT.

ABBATIA S. PETRI JUXTA VILLAM DE GANDAVIO.

ST. PETER.

Ghent, a city of Auftrian Flanders, and the fee of a bifhop, has an abbey of Benedictine monks, founded about A. D 610, by Sigebert king of Auftrafia, at the requeft of St. Amandus, and reftored about A. D. 946, by Arnold earl of Flanders.

See Hiftoire Generale des Païs Bas, Bruffells, 1720. 12mo. vol. II. p. 38. where there is a beautiful view of the cathedral.

Eltrude, niece to king Alfred, gave the manor of Lewifham in Kent to the abbey of St. Peter at Ghent, many years

years before the Conquest, upon which it became a cell of Benedictine monks to that house. Tanner's Notitia, p. 209. Hasted's Kent, I. 68.

See Domesday in Kent.

Edward III. founded a priory of friers aliens Minorites (Dominicans, according to Philpot) at Greenwich in Kent, which was made a cell to Ghent, and given afterwards to Shene. The manor of Greenwich belonged to St. Peter's abbey at Ghent, not by the gift of Edward III. but of more ancient donation, being part of the endowment of their cell at Lewisham, and with that was settled upon Shene. Weever, p. 339. Tanner's Notitia, p. 227. Hasted's Kent, I. 14.

Monasticon, tom. I. p. 550.

Rot. Fin. 33 E. III. m. 3.

S. PETER AT ROME.

ST. PETER at ROME.

ECCLESIA ROMANA BEATI PETRI APOSTOLI.

Tenuit de rege Peritone. Eddid regina tenebat tempore regis Edwardi. Ibi funt vi hidæ; fed non geldebat nifi pro v hidis. Terra eft xii carucatarum. De eis funt in dominio iii hidæ, & ibi ii carucatæ, & iiii fervi, & xi villani, & iiii bordarii, cum vi carucis. Ibi cl acræ prati, & cl acræ pafturæ. Redd' per annum xii libras.

Domefday, Somerfetfhire.

ADDENDA.

P. 131. TOURS.

Mr. Clarke, in a letter to Mr. Bowyer, 1743, says, "In an indenture dated 1372, between Ed. III. and John of Gaunt, about the exchange of lands in Sussex, &c. mention is made of *Prioratus de Withyham, qui est cella Abbatiæ St. Martini de Meremest* (or *Meremost*) *Turonen*." He asks, "Is not this story of *Martin of Tours* conquering the hundred of Kemaes merely a Welsh legend? The Welsh History mentions no settlements in Wales before *Robert Fitzhammon* and his knights. But their heads were usually full of heroes; and from a saint, or reformer of an order, they have raised a conqueror of a conntry. I know Camden tells this story; but he tells it from Welsh Antiquaries, and they have no great weight with me."

APPENDIX.

No. I.

An Account of Priories Alien belonging to King's College in Cambridge, &c. referring to the Notitia Monastica of Dr. Tanner, 8vo edition, 1695. Transcribed from Harleian MS. 7048. p. 65.

The pages in hooks refer to the 2d or folio edition.

Notitia Mon. p. 8. 82. [17 ed. fol.]

Stratfield Say priory is rightly placed in Berks, and now belongs to Eton college. The next parish is called Stratfield Sea, but in Hants.

P. 11. [67] The deanry of St. Burien was given by Henry VI. to King's college in Cambridge. Lit. Pat. Hen. VI. penes præpositum et scholares Coll. Regal. Cant. The bishop of Exeter now holds it in commendam of the crown*. Additions to Camden, in Cornwall, p. 20.

P. 31. [68] St. Michael's Mount was given by H. VI. to King's college in Cambridge, but Sion abbey got it from them. Lit. Pat. H. VI. penes eosdem.

P. 45. [92] The Cluniac priory of St. James at Exeter, founded by Baldwin

---

* This is a strange mistake, for it has been, as it always was, an independent deanry in the gift of the crown: the present dean is the rev. Dr. Nicholas Boscawen, brother to Lord Falmouth, appointed 1756.

de Riveriis, earl of Devon, was made a priory alien by Maud the empress, and given by her to St. Martin de Campis in Paris. Mon. Angl. tom. I. p. 644. Henry VI. and Edward VI. gave the revenues of it to King's college in Cambridge, who have enjoyed them ever since. Lit. Pat. Hen. VI. & Edw. IV. penes præpositum et scholares Coll. Regal. Cant. This priory was not in Exeter, but about a mile distant. All the monks with the prior were but few in number, and consequently this could not be that priory, worth (26 H. VIII.) £.502. 12s. 9d. Mon. Angl. tom. I. p. 1025*. This priory is left out of

* The reference should be p. 1039, where Dr. T. in 2d edition, p. 92, n. g. supposes it should be read £.102. 12s. 9d. and that St. *John's* priory in this city was intended.

the catalogue of the priories alien, ſuppreſſed 2 Hen. V. by the editors of the Monaſticon Anglicanum.

P. 55. [106] Stower Preaux was an alien priory belonging to the nuns of St. Leger de Preaux in Normandy, given by Roger Beaumont conceſſu Willelmi Regis Expugnatoris Anglorum. Rogerius de Bellmonte Rotberti comitis Mellenti et Legreceſtriæ, qui dedit prioratum de Toftes monachis Sti. Petri de Preaux. Neuſtria Pia, p. 524. Henry VI. and Edward IV. gave this priory and manor to King's college, Cambridge. Lit. Pat. Hen. VI. & Edw. IV. penes Coll. Regal Cant.

P. 84. [169] It ſhould not be Andover, but Andwell, which lies between Baſingſtoke and Hartford-bridge.

P. 150.

APPENDIX.

P. 150. [345] Toftes, a priory alien belonging to the monks of St. Peter de Preaux in Normandy. Henry VI. gave the priory to Eton college; but Edward IV.* to King's college in Cambridge. Neuſtria Pia, p. 516. Mon. Angl. tom. III. p. 2. 198. Lit. Pat. Edw. IV. penes præpoſitum & ſcholares Coll. Regal Cant.

P. 155. [342] Leſſingham was an alien priory belonging to Bec in Normandy. Gerard de Guernſey † gave the manor or priory, or both, to thoſe monks. Mon. Angl. tom. II. p. 954. Henry VI. gave this priory to Eton college. Mon. Angl. tom. III. p. 2. 198. Edward IV. gave it to King's

* See Edward the Fourth's charters to King's college and Eton in the Rolls of Parliament.

† Gournay.

college in Cambridge. Lit. Pat. E. IV. penes Coll.

P. 211. [512] Brisete was a priory of the order of St. Austin, founded by Ralph Fitz Brian, temp. H. I.; but afterward made a priory alien by William bishop of Norwich, who annexed it to the priory de Nobiliaco (Lemovien. dioc.) i. e. in the diocese of Limoges in France, viz. in the dutchy of Berry. Carta Will'i Ep'i Norwic. penes Coll. Regal. Cant. Jos. Scaligeri Galliæ Notitia. Vide Catalogum Prioratuum Alienig. suppressor. 2 Hen. V. Mon. Angl. tom. 1. p. 1035. where Brisete is put among the priories alien then suppressed, but no mention made to what priory beyond sea it belonged.

Henry

APPENDIX.

Henry VI. gave the revenues of Brifet priory to King's college in Cambridge. Lit. Pat. Hen. VI. penes præpofitum et fcholares Coll. Regal.

P. 215. [524] Kerfey was a priory of canons of the order of St. Auftin. Sir Henry Grey, lord Powis, gave this priory, and all the revenues of it, to King's college, Cambridge, purfuant to an act of parliament made 24 Hen. VI. V. Cartam Henrici Grey militis d'ni Powis penes eofdem dat. 16 Mar. 25 Hen. VI.

P. 229. [572] Wotton Wawen, a priory alien belonging to the abbey of St. Peter de Conches in Normandy, to which it was given by Robert de Tony & Nic. de Stafford. Monaft. Angl. tom. I. p. 558.

Henry

Henry VI. and Edward IV. gave all that part of the revenues of this priory, which Robert de Tony and Nic. de Stafford gave to King's college, Cambridge, together with the manors of Mockley in Warwickſhire, and Weſt Wrotham in Norfolk, both belonging to this priory. Lit. Pat. Hen. VI. & Ed. IV. penes Coll. Reg. Cant.

P. 239. [599] Okeburn was the richeſt cell in England, belonging to Bec in Normandy. Henry VI. gave the reverſion of the priory, and both the manors of Okeburn magna and Okeburn parva, to the univerſity of Cambridge, who ſoon after ſurrendered their right to the reverſions; and then he gave the priory and two

two manors of Okeburn, and alſo many other manors belonging to Okeburn priory, to King's college, Cambridge.

Edward IV. confirmed the grant of John duke of Bedford of the tithes of Okeburn, to the dean and canon of Windſor, who now enjoy them, and no more. Carta H. VI. penes Coll. Regal. Cant. Carta Cancellarii et Univerſ. Cant. penes eoſdem. Lit. Pat. Hen. VI. penes eoſdem. Monaſt. Angl. tom. III. p. 2. 71.

No. II.

Lands and Poffeffions of Alien Priories given by Henry VI. a. r. 20. 1442, to his College at Eton. Mon. Ang. III. part II. p. 197. Rot. Parl. 20 Henry VI. vol. V. p. 47.

CAMBRIDGESHIRE.

A yearly penfion of 40 s. from Fulbourne church to Pantfield priory, Effex.

ESSEX.

The tithes of St. Mary Berwes * in Effex.

A yearly rent of 12 marks from Montacute priory.

MONMOUTHSHIRE.

Another of 20 s. from Goldcliffe priory.

* Quære Buers in Suffolk.

NORFOLK.

£.16. rent from Edmund Clere, esq. for Leffingham priory.

Reverfion of Horftede manor, held by William lord Bardolf.

Rent of 20 marks paid by Dr. Tho. Tuddenham for Dokkyng priory.

The priory and manor of Toftes cum pertinentiis.

£.30. annual rent from Sir William Philip, for Cretyng and Everden priories, in Suffolk and Norfolk.

Priory of Sporle cum pertinentiis.

Rent of 13*s*. 4*d*. from Thetford priory to the abbey of Cluni.

Rent of £.70. 12*s*. from Sir John Steward, for the manor of Eftwortham in Norfolk, and Bledlow, Bucks.

GLOUCESTER.

£.53. 6*s*. 8*d*. rent from the manors of Bekford priory in Gloucester and Lincolnshire.

Brymmesfield priory.

Yearly rent of £.11. paid by Sir Robert Roos, for the lands of the alien priory of Bailbek *.

SUFFOLK.

Blakenham manor, parcel of Okeburn priory, Wilts.

MIDDLESEX.

Reversion of a house and a shop in St. Botolph's parish, Aldersgate, [*Archychegate* Mon. Ang.] London.

OXFORDSHIRE.

Cotesford manor, parcel of Okeburn priory, Wilts.

* The Cistertian abbey of Beaubec in Normandy.

100*s*.

100 *s*. rent from John Iwardby and Joan Lynde, for the portion of the prioress of Clarevaux *(de Claro Rivolo)* in Mapilderham church.

Rent of £.8. 13 *s*. 8 *d*. paid by William lord Lovell to the crown, for Mynstre Lovell priory.

34 *s*. rent from William York for a water-mill, &c. at Goryng, parcel of Okeburn priory, cell to Bec priory.

£. 13. 6 *s*. 8 *d*. from lord Lovell for Cogges priory.

DEVON.

Modbury priory cum membris & pert.

BERKS.

11 marks rent from John Chafer and John Bermyngham, clerk, for Stratfield Say priory.

SOMERSET.

£.7. from Henry Barette, for parcels at Endeston late belonging to St. Sever priory.

£.25. 6s. 8d. from Robert Vise, monk, and Walter Sergeant, for Stoke Courcy priory.

DORSET.

£.14. 8s. 4d. from Robert Parsite, clerk, for the manor of Hynepiddle (Pidelhinton), late belonging to Mortaygne priory *.

£31. 6s. 8d. from Robert Chauntery, parson of Longbridy, for the revenues of Sturminstre. Marshall church, late parcel of the hospital of St. Giles at Pont Audomar †.

* Hutchins' Dorsetsh. I. 578.
† Ibid. II. 132.

SURRY.

£.19. rent from John Arderne, esq. for the manor of Totyngbek.

Reversions of rents, &c. after the death of Humphrey duke of Gloucester, the king's uncle, in the following places, viz. 2 marks pension out of Horsham St. Faith's, Norfolk, due to the abbey of Conches; 40s. from Tikford priory, by Newport Pagnel, Bucks; £.4. from Folkston priory; £.26. 13s. 8d. besides £.11. 6s. 8d. from Darlegh priory; £.7. 18s. 5d. from Southwik priory, Hants, for Colemere.

SUSSEX AND HANTS.

£.23. 16s. 4d. from Sir Roger Fenys, treasurer of the houshold, for the manor of Hoo and Preston.

£.5. 13s. 2d. rent from Walter Strikland, esq. for lands, &c. in N. Mundam, Compton and Welegh, late parcel of Lucerne abbey in Normandy.

Reverſion of 100s. from the prior of Lewes.

Reverſion of Leomynſtre priory, Suſſex, held by Walter Strikland, esq.

£.8. from Walter Veer, esq. for St. Elen's priory in the Iſle of Wight.

9 marks and 4d. from John Arderne, esq. and Walter Eſton, clerk, for Elyngham priory.

WILTS.

£.40. from Walter Everard and Richard Tourbre, for Clatford priory (misprinted in the Rolls Chatford).

£.22. from John Staunford of Rinhale, for Charleton manor.

Lands

APPENDIX.

Lands and Poffeffions of Alien Priories granted by H. VI. to his College of St. Mary and St. Nicholas (now KING's COLLEGE) in Cambridge, at different Times, confirmed 1444, a. r. 23.

WILTS.

The manor of Great and Little Okeburne, parcel of the priory there.

Manor of Brighton Deverell, parcel of the fame.

100 *s*. rent out of the lands of the abbey of Lucerne, after the death of his uncle, Humphrey duke of Gloucefter.

Reverfion of Willoughton manor, belonging to St. Nicholas abbey at Angiers.

Reverſion of John Merſhton's penſion of 100 s. out of Weſt Kington, in the archdeaconry of Wilts, and deanery of Malmſbury, late belonging to Foulgeres abbey.

Profits of Coſham church, late belonging to St. Nicholas abbey, Angiers.

YORK.

Reverſion of Allerton Mauleverer priory.

NOTTINGHAM.

Reverſion of £. 20. penſion from the abbat of Rufford, for the moiety of Rotheram church, paid to the abbat of Clarevaux.

40 s. from the prior of Blythe, paid to their foreign houſe, (viz. the abbey of St. Katherine near Rouen).

SALOP.

Reversion of 100 s. rent from Wenlok priory.

HANTS.

Reversion of the manors of Monkeston and Combe.

An acre of land in Ringwood.

DORSET.

Reversion of the priory and manor of Stour Preaux, paid to St. Leger de Preaux abbey, Normandy.

CORNWALL.

Priory of Mount St. Michael.

Deanry of St. Burian, belonging to the alien priory there *.

---

* The deanry, as alien, was given 24 Hen. VI. to King's college, Cambridge, and afterwards by king Edward IV. (anno regni 7) to Windsor college, yet neither

Manor of Tylefhide, parcel of the abbey of Caen.

ESSEX.

Felfted manor and rectory, late parcel of Caen abbey.

LINCOLN.

Lands of St. Nicholas abbey at Angiers, in Spalding, Pynchbec, and Repynghale.

LANCASHIRE.

Advowfon of Preftcote church.

SUFFOLK.

Brifet priory, and all its poffeffions.
Kerfey priory, and all its poffeffions.

neither of thofe focieties long enjoyed or had any benefit from it; for it was all along, and ftill continues, an independant deanry, in the gift of the crown, or of the duke of Cornwall, of exempt jurifdiction as a royal free chapel. Tanner, Notit. p. 67.

No. III.

APPENDIX.

No. III.

FORMS OF INDENIZATION OF ALIEN PRIORIES.

1. Petition of THETFORD ABBEY to be made Denizon.

Reyner de Antiq. Benedict. in Angliæ,

Appendix tertiæ partis, p. 209. Scriptura lxxxi.

Ex Archivis Turris Londinenfis. Ex Bundello Petitionum Parliamenti temp. Ed. III.

Regi noftro maxime tremendo.

Supplicant humiliter ejus pauperes fideles oratores prior et conventus monachorum Thetfordiæ ordinis Cluniacenfis, quod cum antehac collatione dicti prioratus pertinente ad abbates Cluniacenfes, priores et plurimi alii mo-

monachi in eo exiftentes fuerint alienigenæ, et ita dicta domus reputata fuerit alienigena, nunc autem evenerit ut prior omnefq. monachi dicti loci fint legales et veri Angli nati et nutriti intra regnum, et nihil apportent extra, et auxilio Dei et aliquorum devotorum fecularium qui fumtus fecerunt, dicti pauperes religiofi acquifiverint et impetraverint liberam electionem fibi et fucceffloribus fuis perpetualiter habendam; et quod prior femper conformetur hic, abfq' eo quod mare tranfire debeat, ita ut deinceps dictus prioratus femper manfurus fit, fi Deo placeat, totaliter fub gubernatione et adminiftratione perfonarum, qui fint veri et legales Angli, placeat vobis propter Deum, et in opus charitatis,

et

et in relevationem dictæ paupercula
domus, quæ propter simplicitatem, et
minus cautam gubernationem priorum
et aliorum monachorum alienigenarum, qui in ea fuerint, et propter
grandia onera superimposita ei illorum
tempore, fere annihilata fuit, et ad
destructionem perducta, ordinare et
stabilire in hoc præsente parliamento,
quatenus deinceps ipsa domus reputetur denizata et libera in omnibus casibus; quodq' nullum onus aut impositio in ullo tempore venturo imponatur aut tanquam debitum exigatur a
dicta domo, nisi tantum eo modo quo
fit aliis domibus religiosis regni nostri
Anglicis et denizatis, seu Anglicani
juris libertate fruentibus.

A nostre

A noſtre treſredote S'r le Roy.

Supplient humblement ſes poveres lieges oratours les priour et convent de moynes de Thetford de l'ordre de Cluny, que comme avant ces heures la collaciun de la dite priorie appartenante as abbey de Cluny, les priours et pluſeurs autres des moynes eſteants en icelle ayent eſte perſonnes alienes, et que ſy la dite meiſon ayt eſtee reputee aliene, et ore ſoyt, enſy que le priour et tous les moynes en dit lieu ſoient loyalx et vray Anglois nees et norriz dedens le royalme, et rien ne apportent par dela, et par l'ayde de Dieu et de aſcunes perſonnes ſeculars qu'ount de leur bonne devocion fait les cuſtages, les dictes poveres religieux ont

ont acquis et impetrez franche eleccion a avoir a eux et a leur fucceffours a tous jours, et que leur priour fera toujourz conferme pardecea fanz paffer la mer, enfy que la dicte priorie deformes demorera toutdiz, fi Dieu pleft, tout entierement fous gouvernance et adminiftration des perfonnes vrays et loyalx Englois, il vous plefe pur Dieu, et en oever de charite, et en relevacion de la dite povere mefon, laquelle par fimpleffe et meynes aviffec governaunce des priours et autres moynes alienes qui y ount efte, et par les grandes charges furmifes a icelle en lour temps, a efte bien pres anyente, et mys a deftruction, ordiner et eftablir ores en cefte prefent parlement, que deformes elle foit tenue et reputee denizein en tous cas, et que nulle charge ne impofition

pofition ne foit en nul temps avenyr mys ne chalengee deuc fur la dicte mefon, fors que enfy come fera d'autres mefons religieux du noftre royalme vrays Anglois et denizennes.

2. INDE-

2. INDENIZATION of the BENEDICTINE Priory of St. TRINITY, YORK.

Rot. Parl. 4 Hen. VI. n. 25. vol. IV. p. 302.

ITEM, une Petition fuit baille a n're Sr le Roi en mefme le Parlement, pur les Priour & Convent de la Priorie de Seint Trinite d'Everwyk, de l'ordre de Seint Benet; le tenour de quele cy enfuit.

Au Roi n're foveraigne S'r. Supplient humblement voz povres ligees & oratours, le Priour & Convent de le Priorie de Seint Trinite d'Everwyk, de l'ordre de Seint Benet, le quel Priorie eft celle de l'Abbaye de Meremoftier en le Roialme de Fraunce: Que come le dit Priorie eft, & a efte avaunt ces heures, un Priorie alien conventuell,

conventuell, qui est, & a este charge de un annuite de XL s̃. p̃ an, a paier annuelment a vous, a v're escheqer, a cause d'une ancien apporte a la chief meason de Meremostier suisdit, durant les guerres pentre les Roialmes d'Engleterre & de Fraunce; la quele annuite & ancien apporte, a cause de la Paix finall faite pentre les Roialmes avauntditz, en ley est expire & determine. Qu'il please a v're tres soveraigne & benigne grace, al reverence de Dieu, & augmentation du divine service en le dit Priorie, & encresse de mesme le Priorie, de graunter as ditz Priour & Convent, p̃ auctorite de cest present Parlement, q'ils, & lour successours, soient deinzeins, & pour deinzeins soient reputez, tenuz & tretez,

en

en mesme le manere & auxi franchement & entierment en toutz choses, sicome autres Priours Englois deinz le Roialme d'Engleterre sont. Et q̄ les ditz Priour & Convent, & lour successours, desore en avaunt aient & tiennent le dit Priorie, ovec toutz lour appurtenaunces, en perpetuitee, come Priorie Englois & deinzein, & discharge du dit apport & annuite envers vous & voz heirs & successours, a toutz jours. Et auxi, q'ils aient toutz les libertees, franchises, immunitees & privileges, & les enjoisent franchement, sicome hommes de religion neez Englois les ount & les enjoisent en toutz points, sicome Priours & Priories Englois de mesme l'ordre deins le Roialme d'Engleterre sount

tretez

tretez & gouvernez, en paiant les difmes, fubfidees & autres devoirs, ficome autres deinzeins de lour ordre deinz le dit Roialme fount & paient. Et outre ce, p auctorite de mefme ceſt Parlement, de graunter as ditz Priour & Convent, q̃ qant, & a quel temps avient q̃ le dit Priorie fe voide p mort, refignation, ou ceffer del Priour de le Priorie fuifdit, ou en autre manere quelconq̃, q'adonq̃ le dit Convent, en chefcune finguler voidance de mefme le Priorie, aient franc election de eux mefmes, d'un de eux eflire en le Pri-our, fanz afcun licence ent avoir ou demander de vous, ou de voz heirs pour toutz jours, pour Dieu & en oevere de charite.

La quele Petition, devaunt les Seign'rs efpirituelx & temporelx du dit
Parlement

APPENDIX.

Parlement leuz & entenduz, a l'efpeciall requeſt des communes de meſme le Parlament, fuit reſponduz en la forme enſuant.

Soient lettres patentes du Roi faitz defouz fon graunde feal fur la contenue de cefte Petition, pur un refonable fyn ent a faire en la Chauncerie du Roy.

No. IV.

De Terris Alienigenarum, propter guerram in Ducatu Aquitaniæ motam, in manum Regis captis eifdem nunc reddendis.

From Rymer, vol. IV. p. 246.

A. D. 1327. 1 E. III. *Clauf.* 1 E. III. *p.* 1. *m.* 22.

REX Thefaurario & Baronibus de Scaccario, Salutem.

Supplicavit nobis dilectus nobis in Chrifto, Prior de Neuport Paynel, quæ eft cella Abbatiæ Majoris Monafterii Turonenfis, per petitionem fuam coram nobis & concilio noftro exhibitam, quòd, cum Dominus E. nuper Rex Angliæ, pater nofter, occafione guerræ, inter ipfum & Regem Franciæ motæ in Ducatu Aquitaniæ, terras,

APPENDIX.

ras, tenementa, feoda & advocationes ad Prioratum prædictum spectantia, simul cum aliis terris, tenementis, feodis, & advocationibus religioforum alienigenarum de poteſtate dicti Regis Franciæ exiſtentium in regno noſtro capi feciſſet in manum ſuam, unà cum bonis, & catallis ejuſdem Prioris in eiſdem terris & tenementis exiſtentibus:

Et terras & tenementa ad Prioratum prædictum ſpectantia, præfato Priori, per litteras patentes dicti patris noſtri ſub ſigillo Scaccarii prædicti conſignatas commiſiſſet tenenda ad voluntatem ſuam, pro quâdam certâ firmâ ſibi indè annuatim reddendâ; feodis militum, & advocationibus eccleſiarum ſibi retentis:

Et etiam tradidisset præfato Priori bona, & catalla prædicta, per certam manucaptionem ad respondendum indè dicto patri nostro ad voluntatem suam:

Velimus eidem Priori dicta terras, tenementa, feoda, & advocationes, unà cum bonis & catallis prædictis, restituere, & arreragia firmæ suæ prædictæ sibi pardonare:

Nos, de assensu Prælatorum, Comitum, Baronum, & aliorum Magnatum, in instanti Parliamento nostro existentium, volentes præfato Priori gratiam facere specialem, reddidimus eidem Priori terras, tenementa, feoda, & advocationes prædicta, unà cum bonis, & catallis supradictis, & hac vice, de gratiâ nostrâ, pardonavimus ei arreragia firmæ suæ prædictæ:

Et

APPENDIX.

Et ideò vobis mandamus quòd præfato Priori omnia terras, tenementa, feoda, & advocationes, ad Prioratum prædictum spectantia, quæ occasione prædictâ in manu dicti patris nostri capta fuerunt, unà cum bonis, & catallis prædictis, sine dilatione liberari, & ipsum de firmâ prædictâ & arreragiis ejusdem, ipsumque, & manucaptores suos de bonis & catallis prædictis exonerari & quietos esse faciatis; salvo nobis apporto Abbatiæ prædictæ de prædicto Prioratu debito, quousque aliud super hoc duxerimus ordinandum.

Teste Rege apud Westmonasterium quarto die Februarii.

Per Petitionem de Concilio.

Consimilia

Confimilia Brevia habent fubfcripti; videlicet,

Abbas de Fifcampo in Normann.

Abbatiſſa de Cadomo* in Normann.

Prior de Wangeford de ordine Clunyacen.

Prior de Horkeſle de ordine Clunyacen.

Prior de Lynton, cella Abbatiæ Sancti Jacuti in Britann.

Prior de Modbury, cella Abbatiæ Sancti Petri ſuper Dyvam † in Normann.

Prior de Loddres, cella Abbatiæ de Monte Burgi in Normann.

Prior de Frampton, cella Abbatiæ Sancti Stephani in Cadomo * in Normann.

Prior de Oteryngton, cella Abbatiæ Sancti Michaelis in Periculo Maris in Normann.

Prior de Theford, cella Abbatiæ Clunyacen. in Normann.

* Cadamo in Rymer.   † Dynam in Rymer.

Prior

APPENDIX.

Prior de Auebury, cella Abbatiæ Sancti Georgii in Normann.

Prior de Clatford, cella Sancti Victoris in Normann.

Prior de Appledercombe, cella Abbatiæ Beatæ Mariæ de Monte Burgi in Normann.

Prior Sanctæ Elenæ de ordine Clunyacen.

Prior de Pontefracto de ordine Clunyacen.

Prior de Blida, cella Abbatiæ Sanctæ Katerinæ de Monte Rothomag. in Normann.

Prior de Hermodefworth, cella ejufdem Abbatiæ.

Prior de Ecclesfeld, cella ejufdem Abbatiæ.

Prior de Merefeye, cella Sancti Audoeni de Rothomago *.

* Rethomago in Rymer.

Prior de la Seke, cella *Abbatiæ Sancti Florencii de Samuro in Andegavia.*

Prior Trinitatis Eborum, cella *Abbatiæ Majoris Monasterii Turonen.*

Prior de Derhurst, cella *Abbatiæ Sancti Dionisii.*

Prior de Berneftaple ordinis Clunyacen.

Prior de Carfewelle ordinis Clunyacen.

Prior Sancti Jacobi juxta Exon. cella *Prioratus Sancti Martini de Campis Parifiis* *.

Frater Richardus Folyn Procurator Abbatis de Bello Becco† *in Normann.*

Prior de Pembrok in Wall. cella *Abbatiæ de Sagio in Normann.*

Frater Richardus Procurator Prioris de Morteyn in Angl.

Prior de Shireburn, cella *domus Sancti Benedicti de Cyrisi.*

* Parifius in Rymer.   † Besso in Rymer.

Prior

Prior de Eye, cella Abbatiæ de Bernay in Normann.

Prior Sancti Walerici, cella Abbatiæ Sancti Walerici in Pykardia.

Prior de Welscricheston, cella Abbatiæ Sancti Petri super Dyvam* in Normann.

Prior de Lenton, ordinis Clunyacen.

Abbas Clunyacen.

Abbas Sancti Martini de Sagio in Normann.

Prior de Crecynges & de Everdon, cella Abbatiæ de Berniato* in Normann.

Priorissa de Lennerministre, cella Abbatiæ de Almanasche in Normann.

Prior de Coges, cella Abbatiæ de Fiscampo in Normann.

Prior de Noiona de Novo Mercato.

Prior de Okeburn.

Prior de Sancto Neoto.

* Dynam in Rymer.   † Q. Berniaco, or Bernaio.

Prior

Prior de Stokes.
Prior de Stynenton.
Prior de Goldclive*.
Prior de Cowyk.
Prior de Wylesford.
Abbas de Sagio.
Prior de Cameryngham.
Abbas de Lyra.
Prior de Caresbrok qui est cella Abbatiæ de Lyra.
Prior de Hynkcleye qui est cella Abbatiæ de Lyra.
Prior de Tytteleye qui est cella Abbatiæ de Tyrona.
Prior Sanctæ Crucis in Insula Vecta, qui est Cella Abbatiæ de Tyrona.
Prior de Hamele qui est cella Abbatiæ de Tyrona.
Prior de Warham qui est cella Abbatiæ de Lyra.

* Godclyne in Rymer.

APPENDIX.

Prior de Appeltrecombe in Insula Vecta, qui est cella de Monte Burgo.

Prior de Paunfeld & de Welle, qui est cella Abbatiæ de Cadomo* in Normann.

Prior Beatæ Mariæ Lancast. qui est cella Abbatiæ de Sagio in Normann.

Prior de Anedewell qui est cella Abbatiæ de Tyrona.

Prior de Folkeston qui est cella Abbatiæ de Lulleyo† in Normann.

Abbatissa de Gynes in Artois.

Prior de Menstre qui est cella Abbatiæ Sanct Cergi in Angania‡.

Prior de Truerdrayth in Cornub. qui est cella Abbatiæ Sancti Cergi in Angania.

Prior Sancti Michaelis in Cornub. qui est cella Abbatiæ Sancti Michaelis in Periculo Maris in Normann.

* Cadamo in Rymer.
† Q. Lonleio.   ‡ Sic. Q. Andegavia.

No. V.

No. V.

De Domibus Religioforum Alienegenarum, in Holderneffe, in Manum Regis capiendis.

From Rymer, vol. IV. p. 777.

A. D. 1337. 11 *E.* III. *Rot. Vafc.* 11 *E.* III. *m.* 19.

REX dilectis & fidelibus fuis, Johanni de Molyns, Nicholao de Bukelond, & Willielmo del Lounde de Holderneffe, Salutem.

Quia Rex Franciæ congregato in diverfis partibus dominii fui magno navigio gentes noftras per mare tranfeuntes hoftiliter expugnare & capi, & idem navigium cum multitudine hominum armatorum fuper regnum noftrum, ac etiam infulas noftras de Gernefeye* & Jerefeye, mitti

* Gernereye in Rymer.

fecit,

fecit, ad noſtrum, ſi poſſit, dominium ſubvertendum: Qui quidem homines navigii illius fines ipſorum regni ac inſularum noſtrarum pluriès ſunt ingreſſi, homicidia, incendia, & alia facinora, crudeliter perpetrando:

Idémque Rex nichilominus grandem mandavit exercitum convocari, ad invadendum hoſtiliter & occupandum terras noſtras & fidelium noſtrorum in ducato noſtro Aquitaniæ, & nos indè pro viribus exhæredandum: ac mala & facinora hujuſmodi nobis & noſtris, tàm per terram, quàm per mare, indiès inferre nititur, ſuâ malitiâ excreſcente, guerram contra nos voluntariè & contra juſtitiam ſic movendo:

Per

Per quod de concilio nostro ordinavimus quòd terræ, tenementa, beneficia, possessiones, ac bona & catalla quæcúmque omnium Gallicorum, & aliorum de dominio & potestate ipsius regis Franciæ, tàm secularium, quàm religioforum, cujuscúmque status seu conditionis existant, infra regnum nostrum (terris, ac bonis & catallis, hominum Britanniæ dumtaxat exceptis) in manum nostram seisiantur; ita quòd nobis de exitibus terrarum & tenementorum illorum ac de bonis & catallis prædictis respondeatur:

Nos, præmissa cum omni celeritate, quâ fieri poterit, volentes executioni demandari, assignavimus vos, conjunctim & divisim, ad capiendum & seisiendum, ftendum, ac capi & feifiri, per aliquos (quos ad hoc deputaveritis) faciendum, in manum noftram ad certum diem, quem vobis duximus præfigendum, omnes prioratus, domos, beneficia, & alia, religioforum & aliorum alienigenarum prædictorum quorumcúmque, de poteftate & dominio dicti regis, necnon bona & catalla eorundem in partibus de Holderneffe, in comitatu Eborum, tàm, vidilicet, equos & animalia, denarios & jocalia, ac vafa aurea & argentea, & blada in terris crefcentia, quàm alia bona fua quæcúmque, ubicúmque exiftentia, five fuerint infra libertates, five extra, unà cum debitis quæ ipfis in partibus prædictis debentur (exceptis terris & bonis ipforum hominum Britanniæ, ut eft dictum)

dictum) & ad eadem, terras, tenementa, poffeffiones, & loca ac bona & catalla quæcúmque fupradicta, falvo & abfque diftractione aliquâ bonorum eorundem per vos, præfate Willielme, cuftodire faciendum, quoufque aliud indè præceperimus; ita quòd de exitibus terrarum, tenementorum, & locorum prædictorum, ac bonis & catallis, denariis, jocalibus, & debitis antedictis (de quibus in cameram noftram volumus refponderi) nobis per vos, prædicte Willielme, in eâdem camerâ noftrâ valeat refponderi: falvâ tamen viris religiofis, miniftris & fervientibus fuis neceffariis, rationabili fuftentatione fuâ, quam ipfis per vos, dicte Willielme, de exitibus domorum fuarum volumus, donec aliud indè mandaverimus, miniftrari:

Et

APPENDIX.

Et ad religiosos prædictos infra prioratus & domos suas, salvè et honestè custodiendum:

Et ad inquirendum, tàm per sacramentum proborum & legalium hominum partium prædictarum, tàm infra libertates quàm extra, per quos rei veritas meliùs sciri poterit, quàm aliis viis & modis quibus meliùs expedire videritis, de debitis quæ eisdem religiosis seu aliis prædictis in eisdem partibus debentur, & quæ & cujusmodi debita, & per quos, & de terminis solutionum eorundem:

Nec non ad indenturas inter vos, prædicte Johannes & Nicholae, seu alterum vestrûm, aut à vobis deputandis, & vos, præfate Willielme, de omnibus bonis & catallis, tàm denariis,

riis, jocalibus, & bladis in terris crefcentibus, quàm aliis bonis & rebus, ipforum religioforum, & aliorum alienigenarum prædictorum quibufcumque, ac de pretio eorumdem, & quæ & cujufmodi fuerint, modo debito conficiendas:

Et ad certificandum* tàm nos in cancellariam noftram, quàm in cameram noftram, de bonis & catallis illis, ac debitis prædictis, & tranfcripta indenturarum illarum ibidem mittendum cum celeritate quâ poteftis:

Et ideò vobis, firmiter injungendo, mandamus quòd circa præmiffa, facienda & explenda in formâ prædictâ, cum omni folicitudine & diligentiâ intendatis, omnibus aliis prætermiffis;

* certificandam in Rymer.

ita

APPENDIX.

ita quòd, per veſtri tepiditatem, ſeu negligentiam in hâc parte, dampnum ſeu jacturam nullatenùs incurramus, per quod ad vos materiam habeamus graviter, prout convenit, capiendi:

Et ſcire facietis, ex parte noſtrâ, ſingulis prioribus domorum & locorum prædictorum, in partibus prædictis, ſeu cuſtodibus eorundem, aut eiſdem præſidentibus, quòd ſint, in propriis perſonis ſuis, coram nobis, & concilio noſtro, apud Weſtmonaſterium, die Lunæ proximo poſt feſtum Sanctæ Mariæ Magdalenæ proximò futurum, ad informandum nos, & dictum concilium noſtrum, ſuper aliiquibus eis ex parte noſtrâ exponendis, & ad faciendum ulteriùs quod tunc ibidem contigerit ordinari.

Mandavimus enim vicecomiti noftro comitatûs prædicti, quòd vobis, in præmiſſis omnibus & ſingulis faciendis, pareat, obediat, & intendat, & coram vobis venire faciat tot & tales probos & legales homines de ballivâ ſuâ, tàm infra libertates quàm extra per quos dictum negotium meliùs expediri poterit, quotiens & quando opus fuerit, & ipſum ſuper hoc ex parte noftrâ, feceritis præmuniri.

In cujus, &c.

Tefte rege apud Staunford primo die Julii.

Per ipſum Regem.

Confimilis commiffio fit Johanni de Molyns, Johanni de Langeford, & Nicholao de Bukelond, conjunctim & divifim, in infulâ Vectâ, in comitatu Suthamptoniæ; ita quod dictus Johannes

APPENDIX.

hannes de Langeford bona, &c. custodiat, & de eisdem respondeat in cameram regis, &c. *ut supra mutatis mutandis.*

Teste ut supra.

Per ipsum Regem.

*Consimilis commissio fit diversis de prioratibus, domibus, beneficiis, & locis religiosorum, & aliorum alienigenarum de potestate & dominio regis Franciæ, in Angliâ, Walliâ, & Hiberniâ, in manum regis capiendis.

* Rot. Vasc. 11 Ed. III. m. 15.

No. VI.

No. VI.

De Prioratibus Religioforum reſtituendis.

From Rymer, vol. VI. p. 311.

A. D. 1361. *An.* 35 *E.* III. *Pat.* 35 *E.* III. p. 1. *m.* 14.

REX omnibus, ad quos, &c. Salutem.

Licet nuper prioratum de Monte Acuto, in comitatu Somerſetiæ, occaſione guerræ inter nos & Gallicos tunc motæ, ac omnia terras, tenementa, feoda, & advocationes, ad prioratum illum ſpectantia, inter alios domos & prioratus religioſorum alienigenarum de poteſtate Franciæ, unà cum bonis & catallis in eiſdem prioratibus & domibus exiſtentibus, in manum noſtram

tram ceperimus, & custodiam eorumdem prioribus locorum prædictorum, & aliis, pro certâ firmâ nobis indè reddendâ, per diversas literas nostras patentes commiserimus:

Quia tamen pax inter nos & magnificum principem, regem Franciæ, fratrem nostrum carissimum, jam reformata & publicata existit:

Nos ob honorem Dei & Sanctæ Ecclesiæ volentes dilecto nobis in Christo Priori de Monte Acuto gratiam facere specialem, eidem priori dictum prioratum de Monte Acuto, ac omnia terras, tenementa, feoda, & advocationes, ad prioratum prædictum spectantia, simul cum omnibus bonis & catallis in eo existentibus, restituimus,

mus, habenda & tenenda adeò plenè & integrè ficut ea tenuit ante captionem fupradictam, abfque aliquâ firmâ nobis indè, ratione captionis prædictæ, exnunc reddenda:

Et ipfum priorem & manucaptores fuos de firma prædicta exnunc exoneramus & quietamus per præfentes; arreragiis firmæ illius, fi quæ fuerint de tempore præterito, & debitis, quæ ante captionem fupradictam debebantur, & nondum foluta exiftunt, nobis femper falvis.

In cujus, &c.

Tefte rege apud Weftmonafterium decimo fexto die Februarii.

Per ipfum regem & concilium.

Confimiles literas regis de reftitutione habent alienigenæ fubfcripti, fub eadem datâ; videlicet,

Prior Prioratus de Norhampton.

Prior

APPENDIX.

Prior Prioratus de Arundell, &c.

Prior Prioratus de Cameryngham, qui est cella Abbatiæ de Blanca Landa in Normann.

Prior Prioratus de Otriton, in comitatu Devoniæ, qui est cella Abbatiæ Sancti Michaelis in Periculo Maris in Normanniâ.

Prior Prioratus de Pritewell, in com. Essex.

Prior Prioratus de Sancto Neoto.

Prior Prioratus de Wotton.

Prior Prioratus de Lenton.

Prior Prioratus de Barnestaple, in comitatu Devoniæ.

Prior Prioratus de Bekford.

Prior Prioratus de Wenlock, qui est cella Prioris de Caritate in Regno Franciæ, &c.*

* Caricate in Rymer.

No. VII.

No. VII.

Pro Religiosis Alienigenis, de Licentia Alienandi.

From Rymer, vol. VII. p. 697.

A. D. 1391. *An.* 14 *R.* II. *Pat.* 14. *R.* II. *p.* 2. *m.* 32.

REX omnibus, ad quos, &c. Salutem.

Sciatis quòd de gratia nostra speciali, concessimus & licentiam dedimus, pro nobis & hæredibus nostris quantum in nobis est Abbati Monasterii Sancti Trinitatis in Monte Sanctæ Katerinæ juxta Rothemagum, & conventui ejusdem loci, de potestate Franciæ, quòd ipsi dare possint, concedere, & assignare, venerabili in Christo patri, Willielmo de Wykeham, episcopo Wyntoniæ, hæredibus & assignatis

natis suis imperpetuum, Maneria de Hermondefworth in comitatu Midds, & Tyngewyk in comitatu Bucks, cum pertinentiis, ac omnia alia ad prædictos abbatem & conventum & eorum monasterium pertinentia, infra regnum nostrum Angliæ, præter prioratum de Blithe, cum pertinentiis : quæ quidem maneria & alia supradicta in manu nostra, occasione guerræ inter nos & adversarium nostrum Franciæ, existunt, & quæ (exceptis feodis militum & advocationibus ecclesiarum & vicariarum in manibus nostris remanentibus) dimittuntur ad firmam per nomen custodiæ prioratûs de Hermondesworth, & omnium terrarum, tenementorum, reddituum, & possessionum ad dictum prioratum spectantium,

tantium, pro qua quidem cuftodia quaterviginti marcæ nobis redduntur per annum : habenda & tenenda prædicta maneria, cum pertinentiis, & prædicta omnia alia, ad prædictos abbatem & conventum & monafterium fuum prædictum infra regnum noftrum Angliæ pertinentiæ (præter prioratum de Blithe cum pertinentiis) præfato epifcopo, hæredibus & affignatis fuis imperpetuum, adeò plenè & integrè ficut prædicti abbas & conventus, vel prædeceffores fui ea unquam habuerunt, feu habere debuerunt, de confuetudine, vel de jure, & adeò quietè, exonerata de firma prædicta, & de omnibus aliis firmis, redditibus, decimis, & aliis quibufcúmque, erga nos & hæredes noftros,

tros, prout prædicti abbas & conventus seu eorum prædecessores ea habuerunt vel tenuerunt antequam ad manus nostras, seu ad manus progenitorum nostrorum, occasione guerræ, devenerunt: et præfato episcopo quòd ipse prædicta maneria de Hermondsworth & Tyngewyk, cum pertinentiis, & omnia alia prædicta, ad ipsos abbatem & conventum & monasterium suum prædictum infra regnum nostrum Angliæ pertinentia (præter prædictum prioratum de Blithe cum pertinentiis) a præfatis abbate & conventu recipere possit, habere & tenere prædicto episcopo, hæredibus & assignatis suis imperpetuum, sicut prædictum est.

Tenore præsentium similiter licentiam dedimus specialem, non obstantibus

tibus aliquo præmiſſorum, ſeu cauſis vel materiis ſupradictis, & eo non obſtante quòd prædicta maneria cum pertinentiis, & alia ſupradicta, ad ipſos abbatem & conventum infra regnum noſtrum pertinentia, de nobis tenentur in capite, ſeu fuerunt de dono vel collatione progenitorum noſtrorum, aut eo quòd fuerunt data per nos vel per progenitores noſtros prædictis abbati & conventui, ſeu eorum prædeceſſoribus, ad cantarias, hoſpitalitatem, opera caritatis, & alia onera facienda, invenienda, ſeu ſuſtinenda, aut aliâ cauſâ quacumque, quæ nos tangit, ſeu nos vel hæredes noſtros tangere poterit quovis modo.

In cujus, &c. Teſte rege apud Weſtmonaſterium decimo die Martii.

Per Breve de Privato Sigillo.

No. VIII.

APPENDIX.

No. VIII.

De Restauratione Prioratuum Alienigenarum.

From Rymer, vol. VIII. p. 101.

A. D. 1399. *An.* 1 H. IV. *Pat.* 1 H. IV. *p.* 2. *m.* 13.

REX omnibus ad quos &c. Salutem;

Sciatis quòd nos intimè considerantes qualiter nonnulla prioratus, domus, & loca religiosa alienigenarum, infra regnum nostrum Angliæ & Walliæ existentia, per nobiles progenitores nostros, ac alios regni nostri proceres & magnates, ad divina officia ac hospitalitatis & eleemosinarum, aliaque pietatis & devotionis onera facienda & supportanda laudabiliter

biliter fundata & conftructa extiterunt: quódque eadem prioratus, domus, & loca religiofa, tàm per fubitas & frequentes ammotiones & expulfiones priorum & occupatorum locorum prædictorum, quàm per diverfos feculares & alios firmarios eorumdem, poftquam in manum domini E. nuper regis Angliæ avi noftri, occafione guerræ inter nos & illos de Francia motæ, primò feifita fuerunt, ita enormiter, tàm in domibus, quàm in rebus & poffeffionibus, deftruuntur, dilapidantur & devaftantur, quòd divinus cultus regularefque obfervantiæ inibi ceffant, ac hofpitalitates, & eleemofinæ, & alia infuper caritatis opera, ibidem ftabilita & fieri confueta fubtrahuntur,

trahuntur, necnon pia fundatorum vota multipliciter defraudantur & frustrantur, ad Dei omnipotentis offensam & displicentiam non modicam ut speramus: Et volentes proindè, ad honorem Dei ac sanctæ ecclesiæ, pro divini cultûs augmentatione, ac dictorum operum caritativorum & aliorum onerum incumbentium innovatione & continuatione, gratiosiùs providere: De gratiâ nostrâ speciali, & ex certa scientia nostra, & de assensu concilii nostri, in præsenti parliamento, manum nostram de prioratu Sanctæ Mariæ Magdalenæ de Barnstapel Exoniensis diocesis; in quo quidem prioratu Simon Ocle, prior admissus, institutus, & inductus existit, sicut per literas admissionis, institutionis, & inductionis

ductionis hujufmodi, nobis in cancellaria noftra exhibitas & oftenfas, plenè liquet; qui quidem prioratus in manum dicti avi noftri, inter alias terras & tenementa religioforum alienigenarum, de dominio & poteftate Franciæ exiftentium, in regno noftro Angliæ, & alibi infra dominium & poteftatem noftram, nuper captus & fcifitus extitit, & in manu noftra, occafione prædictâ, exiftit; penitus ammovemus, & eundem prioratum eidem Simoni priori concedimus & reftituimus per præfentes: Habendum & tenendum fibi & fucceſſoribus fuis, prioribus loci prædicti, unà cum omnibus cellis, maneriis, terris, tenementis, redditibus, fervitiis, feodis militum, advocationibus eccleſiarum, vicariarum, capellarum,

&

& cantariarum, & aliorum beneficiorum ecclefiafticorum quorumcumque: ac etiam cum omnibus penfionibus, portionibus, annuitatibus, decimis, obligationibus, eleemofinis, ac aliis emolumentis, proficuis, rebus, & poffeffionibus, tàm fpiritualibus quàm temporalibus, ad prioratum prædictum pertinentibus: Reddendo indè annuatim nobis & hæredibus noftris, durante guerrâ inter nos & illos de Franciæ, antiquum apportum dumtaxat, quod ad capitalem domum prioratûs prædicti in partibus tranfmarinis, tempore pacis, de eodem prioratu reddi & folvi confuevit:

Ita tamen quòd idem prior & fucceffores fui monachos, capellanos feculares, & alios miniftros Anglicos, in prioratu prædicto, ad numerum juxta primariam fundationem ejufdem debitum & confuetum, inveniant & fuftentent; ac decimas, quintafdecimas, & alia fubfidia quæcumque, cum clero & communitate regni noftri Angliæ, quotiens & quando concedi contigerint, nobis & hæredibus noftris, pro fpiritualibus & temporalibus fuis, folvant; aliaque onera & pietatis opera, eidem prioratui ab antiquo incumbentia, faciant & fuftentent, juxta primariam fundationem fupradictam; aliqua ordinatione, in contrarium editâ, feu dicta feifinâ prioratûs prædicti, cum pertinentiis fuis prædictis, in manum dicti avi noftri, aut aliquâ aliâ feifinâ, in manum noftrum, aut præfati avi noftri, feu Richardi nuper regis Angliæ,

gliæ, occasione guerræ prædictæ, inde factâ, seu aliquibus concessionibus & commissionibus, inde, ante hæc tempora, per nos, aut dictum avum nostrum, seu præfatum Richardum nuper regem Angliæ, aliquibus personis ad firmam factis non obstantibus:

Volentes insuper & concedentes, pro nobis & hæredibus nostris prædictis, quòd prædictus prior & successores sui prædicti, de quacumque aliâ firmâ & solutione annuâ, nobis vel hæredibus nostris, pro prioratu prædicto, occasione guerræ prædictæ, præter dictum antiquum apportum annuum dumtaxat, in futurum solvendis, quieti sint & exonerati, ac penitùs absoluti; & eundem priorem, & manucaptores suos, necnon alios quoscúmque, inde indè exoneramus & quietamus per præsentes; proviso semper quòd de arreragiis firmæ prioratus illius, ante datam præsentium debitis, & nondum solutis, si quæ fuerint, nobis respondeatur & satisfiat, ut est justum.

In cujus, &c. Teste rege apud Westmonasterium decimo tertio die Novembris.

Per ipsum regem.

Similar writs were at the same time issued for the several priories following:
Lodres, in the diocese of Sarum.
Mount St. Michael, dioc. Exeter.
Blithe, dioc. York.
The Holy Trinity, dioc. York,
Moddebury, dioc. Exeter.
Andover, dioc. Winchester.
Montacute, dioc. Bath & Wells.
Folkestone, dioc. Canterbury.

Hagh

APPENDIX.

Hagh, dioc. Lincoln.

Lynton, dioc. Ely.

St. Neot's, dioc. Lincoln.

St. Andrew at Northampton, dioc. Lincoln.

Lire Ocle, dioc. Hereford.

The church of the Blessed Mary at Carisbrook in the isle of Wight, dioc. Winchester.

Lapley, dioc. Litchfield & Coventry.

St. James near Exeter, dioc. Exeter.

The Blessed Mary at Monmouth in Wales.

St. Helen in the Isle of Wight, dioc. Winchester.

Tykeford near Newport Pagnell, dioc. Lincoln.

Tuttebury, dioc. Litch. & Cov.

St. Nicholas at Pembroke, dioc. St. David's.

210   APPENDIX.

Monks Kirkeby, dioc. Litch. & Cov.
The Bleſſed Mary at Lancaſter, dioc. York.
Hynckeley, dioc. Lincoln.
The Bleſſed Mary at *Strogullia**, dioc. Landaff.
Totton, dioc. Exeter.
Bergaveny, dioc. Landaff.
Cowyk, dioc. Exeter.
The Bleſſed Mary at Goldeclive †, dioc. Landaff.
Trewerdhayth, dioc. Exeter.
Alverton, dioc. York.

† Strogull, or Strigule.   * Goldeclina in Rymer.

No. IX.

APPENDIX.

No. IX.

Act for suppressing the Alien Priories.

E Rotulis Parliamenti anno secundo Henrici V. apud Leicestriam, No. 9. Rot. Parl. vol. IV. p. 22.

ITEM prient les Communes que en cas que final pees soit pris parentre vous nostre sovereine Seigneur et vostre adversarie de France en temps a venir, et sur ceo toutz les possessions de Priories Aliens en Engleterre esteantz as chiefs maisons de religeouses de par dela, as queux tielx possessions sont regardantz, seroient restituz, damage et perde aviendroient a votre dit roialme et a vostre people de mesme le roialme par les graundes fermes et apportz de monoye quel d'an en an toutz jours apres seroient renduz

duz de mesmes les possessions a les chiefs maisons avaunt ditz a tres graunde enpoverissement de mesme voftre roialme en cel partie, que Dieu defende.

Plese a voftre tres noble et tres gracious Seigneurie, par consideracion suisdit, et auxi par consideracion que a la commencement de la guerre commencee parentre les ditz roialmes, des toutz les possessions queux vos lieges alors avoient des douns de vos nobles progenitours en les parties de par dela deinz la jurisdiction de France, par juggement renduz en mesme le roialme de France sont pur toutz jours ouftez et disheritez ; et sur ceo gracioufement ordeiner en cest present parlement, par assent de vos Seigneurs

Seigneurs Efpirituelx et Temporelx, que toutz les poffeffions des Priories Aliens en Engleterre efteantz purront demurrer es vos mains, a vous & a voz heires pur toutz jours, a l'entent que divines fervices en les lieux avaunt ditz purront pluis duement eftre faitz par gentz Englois en temps a venir que n'ont efte faitz avaunt ces heures en ycelles par gentz Fraunceys; forfpris les poffeffions des Priories Aliens conventuelx, et des priours qui font inducts et inftituz, et forfpris que toutz les poffeffions aliens donez par le tres gracious Seigneur le Roi voftre piere (que Dieu affoille) a le meftre et college de Fodrynghay et a fes fucceffours, de la fundacion de noftre dit Seigneur le Roi voftre piere et la fundacion de Edward duc de York,

York, non obſtant la pees affaire, ſi aſcun y ſerra, oveſque toutz maners fraunchiſes et libertees par noſtre dit Seigneur le Roi voſtre piere grauntez as ditz meſtre et college & a ſes ſucceſſours & par vous confirmez, demurgent perpetuelement par auctorite de ceſt preſent parlement as ditz meſtre et college et ſes ſucceſſours a l'oeps et entent ſelonc le tenure et purport de les lettres patentz de noſtre dit Seigneur le Roi voſtre piere de la fundacion du dit college, ſaunz aſcun charge ou apport a vous tres ſoveraign Seigneur et a voz heires, ou a aſcuny outres perſones ou perſone apportiers; ſavaunt les ſervices duez a les ſeigneurs de ſes Engloys, ſi aſcuns y feroient, non obſtant que meme le

graunte

graunte fait par noſtre ſuiſdit Seigneur le Roi voſtre piere as ditz meſtre et college et a ſes ſucceſſours, ne ſoy extende forſque durant la guerre par entre vous tres ſouverain Seigneur & voſtre adverſarie de Fraunce; & ſavant auxi a cheſcun de voz liegez ſi bien eſpirituelx come temporelx l'eſtat & poſſeſſion q'ils ount a preſent en aſcuns de tieux poſſeſſions aliens, ſoit il purchacez ou a purchacerz en perpetuite ou a terme de vie ou a terme d'ans, de les chiefs maiſons de par dela, par licence de noſtre Seigneur le Roi voſtre tres noble piere (que Dieu aſſoille) ou de Roi Edward le tierce voſtre beſaiel, ou de Roi Richard le Seconde puis le Conqueſt, ou de voſtre tres gracious doun, graunt, confirmation ou licence, euz a preſent en cell parties;

ties: paiantz et fupportantz toutz les charges, penfions, annuitees, et corodies grauntez a afcuny de vos lieges par vous ou afcun de voz nobles progenitours a prendre de les poffeffions ou Priories Aliens fuis ditz.

Le Roi le voet; et auxi que les ditz meftre & college de Fodrynghay eient exemplification du Roi defoutz fon graunde feal d'icefte peticion, pour lour greindre feurete cefte partie, et ceo de l'affent des feigneurs efperituelx et temporelx en cefte prefent parlement efteantz.

No. X.

No. X.

De Prioratibus alienigenis in feodo concessis.

From Rymer, vol. X. p. 802.

A. D. 1440. *Rot. Parl.* 19 *Hen.* VI. *p.* 1. *m.* 30.

REX omnibus, ad quos &c. Salutem.

Sciatis quòd nos fidelitate & circumspectione venerabilium in Christo patrum, Henrici* archiepiscopi, Johannis † Bathoniensis & Wellensis episcopi, Johannis ‡ Assavensis episcopi, & Wiilielmi ∥ Sarum episcopi, ac dilecti & fidelis consanguinei nostri Willielmi comitis Suffolciæ, necnon dilectorum nobis, Johannis Somerseth,

* Henry Chicheley.   † John Stafford.
‡ John Law.   ∥ William Aiscoth.

Thomæ

Thomæ Bekyngton, Ricardi Andrewe, Adæ Moleyns, clericorum, Johannis Hampton, Jacobi Fenys, armigerorum, & Willielmi Trefham, plenius confidentes, & ob grandem fiduciam quam penes prædictas perfonas gerimus & habemus: Dedimus & conceffimus eis omnia & omnimoda illa prioratus, maneria, terras, tenementa, redditus, fervitia, penfiones, portiones, apportus, & poffeffiones infra regnum noftrum Angliæ ac Walliæ & marchias Walliæ prædictæ (quæ nuper prioratus & poffeffiones alienigenarum nuncupantur) alicui domui religiofæ feu aliquibus domibus religiofis in partibus tranfmarinis nuper pertinentia five fpectantia, in manibus noftris exiftentia:

Habenda

Habenda & tenenda fibi, hæredibus & affignatis fuis; fimul cum advocationibus omnimodis illorum prioratuum, rectoriarum, ecclefiarum, vicariarum, capellarum, cantariarum, hofpitalium, & aliorum beneficiorum ecclefiafticorum, quæ ad præfens nuncupantur, feu nuper vocabantur, prioratus & poffeffiones alienigenarum, infra dictum regnum noftrum ac Walliæ & marchias Walliæ prædictæ exiftentibus, alicui hujufmodi domui five aliquibus hujufmodi domibus in dictis partibus tranfmarinis nuper pertinentibus five fpectantibus; fimul etiam cum feodis militum, franchefiis, & libertatibus quibufcumque, præmiffis feu alicui præmifforum qualitercumque pertinentibus five fpectantibus;

VOL. II. P de

de nobis & hæredibus nostris per fidelitatem tantùm pro omnibus servitiis, oneribus, exactionibus, & demandis, a festo Paschæ ultimò præterito imperpetuum :

Concessimus etiam eisdem archiepiscopo, episcopis, comiti, Johanni, Thomæ, Ricardo, Adæ, Johanni, Jacobo, & Willielmo, omnes & singulos redditus & firmas, quos aliqua persona seu aliquæ personæ nobis, pro aliquibus hujusmodi prioratibus, maneriis, terris, tenementis, redditibus, servitiis, pensionibus, portionibus, apportubus, & possessionibus quibuscúmque, reddere tenetur seu tenentur: Habendos & tenendos eosdem redditus & firmas ; simul cum reversionibus tàm eorumdem prioratuum, maneriorum, terrarum,

rum, tenementorum, reddituum, servitiorum, pensionum, portionum, apportuum, & possessionum, cum acciderint, seu qualitercúmque ad manus nostras vel hæredum nostrorum devenire poterunt vel debebunt, quàm quorumcúmque aliorum prioratuum, maneriorum, terrarum, tenementorum, reddituum, servitiorum, pensionum, portionum, apportuum, & possessionum infra dictum regnum nostrum Angliæ ac Walliæ & marchias Walliæ supradictæ, quæ ad præsens, ut præmittitur, nuncupantur seu nuper vocabantur prioratus & possessiones alienigenarum, alicui domui religiosæ seu aliquibus domibus religiosis in dictis partibus transmarinis nuper pertinentes sive spectantes, quos aliqua persona,

persona, seu aliquæ personæ, tenet, habet, seu occupat, tenent, habent, seu occupant, ad terminum vitæ per legem Angliæ, vel in dotem, seu in feodo talliato, seu aliàs ad terminum annorum, aut alio modo quocúmque, ex concessione seu dimissione nostra, vel alicujus progenitorum nostrorum, & quæ per seu post mortem ejusdem personæ, seu earumdem personarum, aut alicujus alterius personæ, seu quavis aliâ de causâ, ad manus nostras, vel hæredum nostrorum, accidere, contingere, reverti, seu remanere poterunt vel debebunt: præfatis archiepiscopo, episcopis, comiti, Johanni, Thomæ, Ricardo, Adæ, Johanni, Jacobo, & Willielmo, hæredibus & assignatis suis, a festo supradicto imperpetuum, de nobis & hæredibus nostris, per fidelitatem tantum pro omnibus servitiis, exactionibus, & demandis:

Eo quòd expressa mentio de vero valore annuo omnium & singulorum præmissorum aut alienjus eorumdem, seu aliorum donorum & concessionum eisdem archiepiscopo, episcopis, comiti, Johanni, Thomæ, Ricardo, Adæ, Johanni, Jacobo, & Willielmo, aut eorum alicui, per nos, aut aliquem progenitorum nostrorum, ante hæc tempora factorum, in præsentibus facta non existit, aut aliquo statuto, ordinatione, seu provisione, perpriùs in contrarium editis, ordinatis, seu provisis, non obstantibus.

In cujus, &c. Teste rege apud castrum suum de Wyndesore duodecimo die Septembris.

Per ipsum regem, & de data prædicta, auctoritate parliamenti.

No. XI.

No. XI.

Pro Decano & Capitulo Ecclesiæ Rothomagensis, super dono & concessione Edwardi Confessoris.

From Rymer, vol. IV. p. 466.

A. D. 1331. *An.* 4 *E.* III. *Pat.* 4 *E.* III. *p.* 2. *m.* 10

REX dilectis sibi in Christo decano & capitulo ecclesiæ Rothomagensis, salutem.

Licet nuper suggesto nobis quòd ecclesiæ de Otery Beatæ Mariæ, Exoniensi diocese, vacabat, & ad nostram donationem pertinuit: Johannem de Charrebrok clericum venerabili patri * J. episcopo Exoniensi præsentaverimus ad eandem:

* James Barkeley.

Quia

APPENDIX.

Quia tamen, per cartas progenitorum nostorum quondam regum Angliæ, & alia diversa munimenta, coram nobis & concilio nostro in instanti parliamento nostro, ex parte vestrâ exhibitas, compertum est quòd vos ex dono & concessione sanctissimi confessoris Edwardi quondam regis Angliæ; interveniente auctoritate diversorum Romanorum Pontificum, necnon archiepiscoporum Cantuariensium, & quorumdam prædecessorum præfati episcopi; ecclesiam illam in proprios usus assecuti fuistis, & eam sic appropriatam tenuistis per longa tempora retroacta: Nolentes vobis, super jure vestro, in hac parte, prætextu dictæ præsentationis nostræ, a nobis, veritate tacitâ, taliter impetratæ, aliquod præjudicium generari,

erari, dictam præsentationem nostram, præfato Johanni ad eandem ecclesiam sic factam duximus revocandam; & vobis nichilominus concedimus quòd pro recuperatione possessionis vestræ ad eandem ecclesiam, a quâ colore dictæ presentationis nostræ amoti fuistis ut dicitur, prosequi possitis in curiâ Christianitatis, quatenùs ad forum ecclesiæ pertinet, non obstantibus præsentatione nostrâ prædictâ seu prohibitionibus nostris, si quæ vobis super hoc delatæ fuerint ex parte nostrâ.

Teste rege apud Westmonasterium vicesimo secundo die Januarii.

[227]

INDEX OF PLACES MENTIONED IN THE SECOND VOLUME.

※※※ The several PRIORIES may be seen in the CONTENTS.

Abbatia Cluniacenses 104, 176, 177, 178, 179.
—— *de Sagio*, 178, 180.
Abbatia Majoris Monasterii Turonensis, 178.
—— *de Bernay* in Normandy, 179.
—— *d'Almanasche* in Normandy, 179.
Abbatissa de Gynes in Artois, 181.
—————— *de Cadamo*, or *Cadomo*, in Normandy, 176, 181.
Abergavenny (Monmouthshire), 102, 210.
Alberbury, or *Abberbury* (Shropshire), 97.
Aldersgate (London), 107.
Allerton Malleverer (Yorkshire), 139, 158.
All Saints St. Mary at Elingham (Hampshire), 4.

All Saints at Stamford, 7.
All Souls College (Oxon), 84.
Alverton (Yorkshire), 210.
Ambrosbury (Wiltshire), 72.
Andover (Hampshire), 144, 208.
Andweile or *Anedewell*, 144, 181.
Apeldercomb, *Appeltrecombe*, *Appledercombe*, or *Appledurwell* (Isle of Wight), 9, 177, 181.
Arundell (Sussex), 195.
Ascot (Buckinghamshire), 68.
Avebury (Wilts), 35, 177.
Axholm (Lincolnsh), 66.
Axmouth (Devonsh.), 10.

B.

Bailbec, or *Beaubec*, in Normandy, 152.
Barnstaple,

INDEX OF

Barnstaple, or *Bernestaple* (Devonshire), 114, 178, 195.
Begare near Richmond (Yorkshire), 129.
Bekford priory (manors in Gloucestershire and Lincolnshire), 152, 195.
Bermondsey (Surrey), 110.
Bernaio, Berniaco, or *Berniato,* (in Normandy), 179.
Bincombe (Dorsetshire), 20.
Bittlesden (Buckinghamshire), 84.
Blakenham (Suffolk), 152.
Blanche Lande, or *Blanca Landa,* (in Normandy), 11, 195.
Bledlow (Bucks), 151.
Blida, Blithe, Blyth, or *Blythe* (Nottinghamshire), 26, 158, 177, 208.
Bordesley (Worcestershire), 120.
Boxgrove (Sussex), 5.
Boxley (Kent), 95.
Bridlington priory (Yorkshire), 88.
Bridport (Dorsetshire), 19.

Bridton (Dorsetshire), 19.
Brighston Deverell (Wiltshire), 157.
Brisete (Suffolk), 146, 160.
Brymmesfield Priory (Gloucestershire), 152.
Burstall Garth, olim *Birstall* (Yorkshire), 38.
Burton Bradstock (Dorsetshire), 19.
Burwell (Lincolnshire), 85.

C.

Cambridge University, 148.
Cameringham (Lincolnshire), 11, 180, 195.
Carisbrook (Isle of Wight), 180, 209.
Carsewelle (Northumberland), 178.
Charleton manor (Wiltshire), 156.
Clatford Priory (Wiltshire), 156, 177.
Coges (Oxfordshire), 179.
Cogges priory (Oxfordshire), 153.
Combe (Hants), 159.

Compton,

Compton, 156.
Cosham church (Wiltshire), 158.
Cotesford (Oxfordshire), 152.
Covenham (Lincolnshire), 100.
Cowyk (Yorkshire), 180, 210.
Crecynges (Essex), 179.
Cresswell, Careswell, or *Kressewell* (Herefordshire), 43, 98.
Cretyng priory (Suffolk), 151.
Cripplegate (London), 107.

D.

De Caritate (the priory of, in France, 195.
Darlegh priory (Derbyshire), 155.
Deerhurst or *Derhurst* (Gloucestershire), 117, 178.
De la Seke, 178.
Dioceses of
  Amiens, 61—63.
  Angers, 64—82.
  Avranches, 52.
  Bayeux, 49—51.
  Beauvais, 83, 84.

Bourdeaux, 85, 86.
Chalons, 87, 88.
Chartres, 89—91.
Coutance, 1—17.
Dol, 92, 93.
Evreux, 43—47.
Ghent, 137, 138.
Langres, 94, 95.
Limoges, 96—98.
Lisieux, 48.
Mans, 99—103.
Mascon, 104—107.
Nevers, 108—110.
St. Omers, 111.
Orleans, 112.
Paris, 113—119.
Perigord, 120.
Poitiers, 121.
Rennes, 122—124.
Rheims, 125—128.
Rouen, 18—42.
Tours, 131—134.
Treguier, 129, 130.
Vienne, 135, 136.
Dokkyng priory (Norfolk), 151.

E.

East Henred (Berksh.), 42.
Eaton College, 81, 118, 130, 141, 145, 150.
Ecclesfield or *Ecclesfold* (Yorkshire), 20, 177.

Edith

Edith Weston or *Edyweston* (Rutlandshire), 34.
Elyngham priory (Hampshire), 156.
Endeston (Somersetshire), 2, 154.
Erskdale (Yorkshire), 44.
Eskdale (Yorkshire), 98.
Estwortham (Norfolk), 151.
Everdon priory (Norfolk), 151, 179.
Eye (Suffolk), 179.

F.

Felsted (Essex), 160.
Fiscamp in Normandy, 176, 179.
Foderinghay College (Northamptonshire), 118.
Folkeston, Folkestone, or *Folkston* priory (Kent), 155, 181, 208.
Frampton (Dorsetshire), 176.

G.

Goldcliffe priory (Monmouthshire), 150, 210.
Goldclive (Monmouthshire), 180.
Goryng (Oxfordshire), 153.

Greenwich (Kent), 138.
Grovebury (Bedfordshire), 71.

H.

Hagh, Halgh, or *Howghe*, on the Mount (Lincolnshire), 14, 209.
Hagham (Lincolnsh.), 2.
Hamele or *Hamebrise* (Hampshire), 93, 180.
Henny (Berkshire), 42.
Hermodesworth or *Hermondsworth* (Middlesex), 26, 177.
Holdernesse (Yorkshire), 182.
HolyCross (Isle of Wight), 180.
Holy Trinity at York, 132.
Hoo and *Preston*, manor of (Sussex & Hants), 155.
Horkesle (Essex), 176.
Horsham, St. Faith's (Norfolk), 155.
Horstede (Norfolk), 151.
Hynkeleye (Leicestershire), 180.

I.

Ipelpen (Devonshire), 122.
Iselham (Cambridge), 93.

K.

K.

Kersey priory (Suffolk), 147, 160.
King's College, Cambridge, 115, 133, 141, 144, 145, 147, 148, 149, 157, 159.
Kirkby or *Monk's Kirkby* (Warwickshire), 65.
Kirkstall (Yorkshire), 39.
Kirstede (Lincolnsh.) 101.

L.

Lancaster, priory of *St. Mary* at, 188, 210.
Langelega, 120.
Lapley (Staffordsh.), 209.
Lappele (Staffordsh.), 126.
Lennerministre (Herefordshire), 179.
Lenton (Nottinghamshire), 106, 179, 195.
Leomynstre priory (Herefordshire), 156.
Leffingham priory (Norfolk), 145, 151.
Lewes (Sussex), 156.
Lewisham (Kent), 137.
Lire Ocle (Herefordsh.), 209.
Lodres or *Loddres* (Dorsetshire), 9, 176.

Lynton (Cambridgeshire), 92, 176, 209.

M.

Mapilderham (Oxfordshire), 153.
Marshall Sturminster (Dorsetshire), 154.
Mepford (Shropsh.), 127.
Mensire, or *Minster*, in the deanry of Trigg Minor (Cornwall), 78, 181.
Merefeye (Essex), 177.
Mockley (Warwickshire), 148.
Modbury or *Moddebury* (Devonshire), 153, 176, 208.
Monkeston (Hants), 159.
Monks Kirkeby (Warwickshire), 210.
Monmouth, 209.
Mons Acutus, or *Montacute* (Somersetsh.), 106.
Montacute Priory (Essex), 150, 208.
Mountgrace, priory of, (Yorkshire), 130.
Mount St. Michael (Cornwall), 159, 208.
Mynstre Lovell priory (Oxfordshire), 153.

N.

N.

Northampton, 194.
N. Mundam (Suffex), 156.
Nun Eaton (Warwickfhire), 71.

O.

Okeburn Great and Little (Wiltfh.), 148. 157. 179.
Oteryngton (Yorkfh.), 176.
Otriton (Devonfhire), 195.
Ovret (Shropfhire), 127.

P.

Pantfield (Effex), 150.
Paunfeld and *de Welle* (Effex), 181.
Pembroke (Wales), 178.
Peritone (Somerfetfhire), 139.
Piddelhinton, or *Hynepiddle* (Dorfetfhire), 154.
Pontefract (Yorkfh.), 177.
Prefcote church (Lancafhire), 160.
Prefton. See *Hoo*.
Pritelwell (Effex), 195.
Pynchbec (Lincolnfh.), 160.

R.

Repynghale (Lincolnfh.) 160.
Riddrefield, now Rotherfield (Suffex), 119.
Rideware (Shropfh.), 127.
Ringwood (Hants), 159.
Rotherham (Nottinghamhamfhire), 158.

S.

St. Andrew, Holborn, 107.
——— at Swavefey (Cambridgefhire), 75.
——— at Minting (Lincolnfhire), 112.
——— at Northampton, 209.
St. Anne near Coventry, 76.
——— at Thirfk (Yorkfhire), 130.
St. Burian or *Burien* (Cornwall), 142, 159.
St. Botolph Alderfgate (London), 152.
St. Cadoc, Monmouth, 80.
St. Elen's (Ifle of Wight), 106, 156, 177, 209.
St. Helier (Jerfey), 15.
St. James without Exeter, 114, 142, 178, 209.
St. John at Exeter, 143.
St. Margaret at Ifeham (Cambridgefhire), 93.
St. Mary at Andover (Hampfhire), 80.
St. Mary Berwes (Effex), 150.

St.

St. *Mary* at Elingham (Hampshire), 4.
St. *Mary* at Hatfield Regis (Essex), 124.
St. *Mary* (Lincolnsh.), 66.
St. *Mary* Magdalen College (Oxford), 82.
St. *Mary* at Monmouth, 80.
St. *Mary* and St. *Nicholas* (Cambridge), 157.
St. *Mary* at Scarborough (Yorkshire), 88.
St. *Mary* at Totness (Devonshire), 76.
St. *Michael's Mount* (Cornwall), 142, 181.
────── (Normandy), 176. 181. 195.
St. *Neot's* (Huntington), 179, 195, 209,
St. *Nicholas* at Bramber (Sussex), 81.
St. *Nicholas* at Pembroke, 209.
St. *Nicholas* at Shoreham (Sussex), 81.
St. *Peter* at Sele (Sussex), 81.
Salisbury cathedral, 9.
Sheen monastery (Surry), 42, 138.
Shireburn (Dorsetshire), 178.
Sion (Middlesex), 9, 142.

Southwell church (Nottinghamshire), 52.
Southwick priory (Hants), 155.
Spalding (Lincolnshire), 66, 160.
Sporle (Norfolk), 81.
Stratford Say (Berks), 141, 153.
Stratfield Sea (Hants), 141.
Stoke Courcy priory (Somersetshire), 151.
Stokes, 180.
Stower Preaux (Dorsetshire), 144, 159.
Sturmenstre (Dorsetshire), 151.
Stynenton, 180.

T.

Takeley (Essex), 63.
Tewksbury abbey (Gloucestershire), 118.
Thetford priory (Norfolk), 151, 161, 176.
Threadneedle-street (London), 135.
Thurlegh, Trewelegh, or *Throuly* (Kent), 111.
Tikford priory (Buckinghamshire), 155.
Toftes Monachorum (Norfolk), 144—145—151.
Tong

Tong College (Shropsh.) 127.
Totness (Devonshire), 76.
Totton (Devonshire), 210.
Totyngbek (Surrey), 155.
Trigtone (Oxfordsh.), 119.
Trinity College (Cambridge, 66.
Trinity priory (York), 167, 178, 208.
Trewerdrayth, Truerdrayth, Truwardraith, or *Tywardreit* (Cornwall), 77, 181, 210.
Tuttebury (Staffordshire), 209.
Tykeford or *Tickford* (Buckinghamsh.), 132, 209.
Tyleshide (Cornwall), 160.
Tyngewyk (Bucks), 28.
Tyttelcye (Herefordshire), 180.

U.

Uphaven (Wiltshire), 20.

W.

Wadene (Dorsetsh.), 50.
Warham (Dorset), 180.
Wangeford (Suffolk), 176.
Weden Pinkney (Northamptonshire), 83.

Welegh (Nottinghamshire), 156.
Welscrickeston, 179.
Wenge, olim *Guinuga* (Buckinghamsh.), 67.
Wenlock (Shropshire), 109, 159, 195.
West Kington (Wiltshire), 158.
West Ravendale (Lincolnshire), 52.
Westwood near Droitwich (Worcestershire), 72.
West Wrotham (Norfolk), 148.
Whitchurch Canonicorum (Dorsetshire), 19.
Wileketone, Willoughton, or *Willyton* (Lincolnshire), 64.
Willoughton manor (Wiltshire), 157.
Wilt (Worcestersh.), 119.
Windsor, dean and canons of, 149.
Windsor College, 159.
Withyham (Sussex), 140.
Wotton, 120, 195.
Wotton Wawen (Warwickshire), 147.
Wylesford (Lincolnshire), 180.
Wytherness (Yorksh.), 39.

F I N I S.

[235]

The EDITOR *is much obliged to a judicious Friend, for pointing out the following* ADDITIONS *and* CORRECTIONS.

In Vol. I.

Page
iv l. 1, 2. *dele* of the religious houses
xlvii l. 11, 12, *read* prebendaries
59, l. 13, *for* abbey *read* priory
78. l. 4, *read* Wawen
149, l. 4, *read* 379

In Vol. II.

29, lin. ult. *for* monks *read* friers
65, l. 5 from the bottom, *read* Wirchia
66, *read* 569
80 lin. ult. *read* 329
81. line 16, *read* fixed at the first of these places.
82. l. 3, erase 559. l. 4, erase 600
44, l. 5, 6, *read* Eskdale. See also the Index.
109, lin. antepen. *read* began at Bermondescy.
135, l. 6, *for* monks *read* canons. See Tanner, p. 314, note c.
142. The text and note may be reconciled by turning to "Kennet's Register and Chronicle," p. 730. Dr. Seth Ward, when bishop of Exeter, procured the deanry of Burien to be settled, after the death of Dr. Weeks, upon the bishops of Exeter for ever. It did not become void till bishop Sparrow's time, who first enjoyed it. The bishops of Exeter were possessed of it till the death of bishop Blackall in 1716; when, by consent of parties, it was made a separate preferment, and given by the prince of Wales to Mr. Harris, the clerk of his closet.
154, l. 9, *read* parfite
178, l. 1, *read* Seie. See Tanner, p. 552, note a.
—— Note, *Parisius*. This word might have retained its place in the text; for Du Cange under this word says, "sine flexu interdum pro ipsa Parisiorum urbe usurpatur." To the instances from foreign writers, there produced, may be added others from our historians; in proof, see Tho. Sprotti Chronica, p. 58, and Chronicon de Dunstaple, p. 202.
180, l. 2, probably Styventon.

BOOKS ON ANTIQUARIAN SUBJECTS,
PRINTED FOR, AND SOLD BY, J. NICHOLS.

I. REGISTRUM ROFFENSE; or, a Collection of ancient Records, Charters and Instruments of divers kinds, necessary for illustrating the Ecclesiastical History and Antiquities of the Diocese and Cathedral Church of ROCHESTER. Transcribed from the Originals by JOHN THORPE, late of Rochester, M. D. F. R. S. and published by his Son JOHN THORPE, Esq. A. M. F. S. A. Together with the monumental Inscriptions in the several Churches and Chapels within the Diocese. *Folio, Price, bound,* 2l. 2s.

II. The First Volume of a new Edition of the BIOGRAPHIA BRITANNICA, published under the immediate Inspection of ANDREW KIPPIS, D. D. *Folio, Price, in boards,* 1l. 11s. 6d.

III. The Connexion of the Roman, Saxon, and English Coins; deducing the Antiquities, Customs, and Manners of each People to modern Times, particularly the Origin of Feudal Tenures and of Parliaments; illustrated throughout with Critical and Historical Remarks on various Authors, both Sacred and Profane. By the late WILLIAM CLARKE, A. M. Chancellor of the Church of Chichester, Residentiary thereof, and Vicar of Amport, Hants. *Quarto, Price, sewed,* 1l. 1s.

IV. An Appendix to Mr. CLARKE's Book, by Mr. BOWYER, 6d.

V. Mr. PEGGE on the Coins of Cunobelin. *Quarto, Price* 3s. *sewed.*

VI. The History of the Town of THETFORD, in the Counties of Norfolk and Suffolk, from the earliest Accounts to the present Time. By the late Mr. THOMAS MARTIN, of Palgrave, Suffolk, F. A. S. *Quarto, Price, in boards,* 1l. 4s.

VII. The History and Antiquities of the Abbey of FURNESS, by the late Mr. WEST. *Quarto, Price, sewed,* 15s.

VIII. Pieces written by M. FALCONET and M. DIDEROT, &c. Translated by W. TOOKE, S. T. P. *Quarto, Price* 4s. *sewed.*

IX. The History of the Royal Abbey of BEC in Normandy, translated from the French MS. of Dom. BOURGET. *Small Octavo, Price* 3s. *sewed.*

X. The Origin of PRINTING, in two Essays, by W. BOWYER and J. NICHOLS. *Octavo, Price* 3s. *sewed.*

XI. A Dissertation upon English Typographical Founders and Foundries, by EDWARD ROWE-MORES, A. M. and A. S. S. With an Appendix, by J. N. 8vo. *Price* 5s. *sewed.* Of this book only EIGHTY COPIES were printed, for private Use.

XII. A Journal from Grand Cairo to Mount Sinai, and back again. Dedicated to the Society of Antiquaries, London. By Bishop CLAYTON. The Second Edition, *Octavo, Price* 2s. 6d.

XIII. Abbé FLEURY's History of the Israelites, *Price* 3s. *sewed.*

In the Press, and speedily will be published,

A Collection of all the WILLS, now known to be extant, of the Kings and Queens of England, Princes and Princesses of Wales, and every other Branch of the Blood Royal, from the Reign of William the Conqueror to that of King Edward the Fourth inclusive. With explanatory Notes and a Glossary.